Valuing Other Voices

Discourses That Matter in Education, Social Justice, and Multiculturalism

Valuing Other Voices

Discourses That Matter in Education, Social Justice, and Multiculturalism

By

Festus E. Obiakor
Sunny Educational Consulting

Information Age Publishing, Inc.
Charlotte, North Carolina • www.infoagepub.com

Library of Congress Cataloging-in-Publication Data

CIP data for this book can be found on the Library of Congress website:
http://www.loc.gov/index.html

Paperback: 978-1-64113-925-0
Hardcover: 978-1-64113-926-7
E-Book: 978-1-64113-927-4

Copyright © 2020 IAP–Information Age Publishing, Inc.

All rights reserved. No part of this publication may be reproduced, stored in a retrieval system, or transmitted in any form or by any electronic or mechanical means, or by photocopying, microfilming, recording or otherwise without written permission from the publisher.

Printed in the United States of America.

CONTENTS

Foreword
    Jacob U'Mofe Gordon vii

Preface ix

1. The Multicultural Fabric of Education in the United States:
In Honor of "E Pluribus Unum" 1

2. Addressing Mythologies That Hamper
Multicultural and Global Education 7

3. How "Special" Is Special Education
for African Americans in the United States 15

4. Leadership for Changing Times 29

5. Beyond Silence in Social Justice and Multiculturalism 33

6. The "Model Minority Myth" and Asians
in America's Higher Education:
Impact on Multicultural Education 39

7. Historically Black Colleges and Universities Matter:
Impact on Teacher Education 47

8. Global Learning and Teaching in General
and Special Education 55

9. Building Self-Concepts of Vulnerable Children and Youth 61

v

vi CONTENTS

10. Benefits of Educating and Hiring an "African"
in America's Higher Education 69

11. "Bandwagon Effect" on Thinking and Society:
Toward Multicultural Problem Solving 89

12. Afterword by Carol Huang 97

References 101

About the Author 109

FOREWORD

Jacob U'Mofe Gordon
Professor Emeritus, University of Kansas,
Kwame Nkrumah Endowed Chair, University of Ghana, 2012–2015

The United States of America has been currently grappling with national leadership crises and issues related to international peace and security; and these challenges have been exacerbated by the recent rise of White supremacy groups, including the Alt-Right Movement and the Ku Klux Klan. Moreover, "tribal" politics in the era of Republican leadership in the U.S. Congress and the executive branch of the U.S. Government have significantly contributed to the problem of national leadership and governance. Unlike never before in recent American history, the stakes are high. As a consequence, all these challenges deserve rigorous analyses.

In *Valuing Other Voices: Discourses That Matter in Education, Social Justice, and Multiculturalism*, Obiakor provides critical and insightful analyses of selected major issues in American life and thought: multicultural education, special education, social justice, global education, leadership, historically Black colleges and universities, children and youth, Africans in American higher education, and global learning and training. This book is a timely, rich, and powerful contribution to the literature in American and global studies. The inclusion of Obiakor's personal experiences in the American academy and society in general makes the book an extremely unique contribution to knowledge. And in so doing, he connects with the rest of us, Black and Brown, and others who have similar experiences with him. Obiakor urges and inspires us to learn from these experiences.

Valuing Other Voices targets primary areas of focus that are intertwined with each other: education and social justice; and then multiculturalism

---

Valuing Other Voices: Discourses That Matter in Education, Social Justice,
and Multiculturalism, pp. vii–viii
Copyright © 2020 by Information Age Publishing
All rights of reproduction in any form reserved.

that is embedded in all. This book provides the necessary foundations for an inclusive educational system that values "equity" and "equality"; the most viable variables for upward mobility in our society. Exploring various dimensions of education including multicultural education and special education, Obiakor identifies gaps in our educational system and provides strategies for change. According to a recent study led by researchers (Chetty, Henderson, Jones, & Porter, 2018) at Stanford, Harvard, and the U.S. Census Bureau, "Black boys raised in America, even in the wealthiest families and living in some of the most well-to-do neighborhoods, still earn less in adulthood than White boys with similar backgrounds" (p. 1). Research also indicates that a defining feature of the "American Dream" is upward income mobility. Sadly, the ideal that children have a higher standard of living than their parents is diminishing; falling from 90% to 50% over the past half century. This book has not only called attention to these and related inequities in the American society, but has also provided a sustainable pathway for a better future.

Another major area of focus in *Valuing Other Voices* that is intertwined with multiculturalism is social justice, a concept of fair and just relations between the individual and society; as measured by the explicit and tacit terms for the distribution of wealth, opportunities, and social privileges. The focus on social justice in America and in the global context is in recognition of the capacity of the American people to organize with others to accomplish ends that benefit the whole global community. The challenge to secure social justice for the most needy and vulnerable among us is well articulated by Obiakor in this book. Clearly, his critical analyses of all the areas of focus in the book are insightful, fascinating, imaginative, thoughtful, provoking, panoramic, and challenging. Thus, American educators and the general public will find this book as a "must read" text. Obiakor has plowed new ground and established a significant scholarly foundation on which to build. I am hoping that by reading and using this book our discourses will improve so that we can make our communities, institutions, states, and nations better places to live.

REFERENCE

Chetty, R., Henderson, N., Jones, M. R., & Porter, S. R. (2018). The Equality of Opportunity Project. Retrieved from www.equalityofopportunity.org

PREFACE

How can we build organizations and institutions that treat people equitably? How can we develop conscientious communities where people's voices are heard and not silenced? How can we go from half truths and alternative facts to real truths that will advance our communities? How can we reduce or eliminate societal ills such as racism, ethnocentrism, xenophobia, religious dogmatism, sexism, homophobia, tribalism, colonial mentality, slave mentality, messiah complex, and terrorism? How can we get into the mind's eyes of others and "treat them as we would like to be treated?" How can we create environments that stimulate fearless or "hearty" conversations between different peoples? How can we learn from history or other people's experiences to make functional goal-directed decisions? And, how can we inspire people to value their differences and similarities as they think and talk in our global village? These are questions that deserve answers in our respective communities, states, nations, and world. This book, *Valuing Other Voices: Discourses That Matter in Education, Social Justice, and Multiculturalism* opens doors of communication for all people willing to create a community, state, nation, or world of harmony. In our world today, we exonerate ourselves and point to others to make the changes that we want. In reality, the changes that we want do not just come and we are the instruments of changes that we want. I agree with the late Dr. Martin Luther King Jr. that:

> Human progress is neither automatic nor inevitable. Even a superficial look at history reveals that no social advance rolls in on wheels of inevitability. Every step toward the goal of justice requires sacrifice, suffering, and struggle, the tireless exertions and passionate concern of dedicated individuals. Without persistent effort, time itself becomes an ally of the insurgent and primitive forces of irrational emotionalism and social destruction. This is

---

Valuing Other Voices: Discourses That Matter in Education, Social Justice, and Multiculturalism, pp. ix–xiii
Copyright © 2020 by Information Age Publishing
All rights of reproduction in any form reserved.

x *Valuing Other Voices*

not time for apathy or complacency. This is a time for vigorous and positive action. (King, 1983, p. 59)

Valuing Other Voices is a book that is based on my experiences as a student, professor, scholar, leader, and professional. Consider this simple, but powerful example! In 1983, as a PhD student at New Mexico State University, in one of our class discussions, a White female student angrily noted: "I hate foreigners, especially the males from Africa and India because they are extremely chauvinistic. They have no respect for women." Our professor and the class were shocked; but, the professor used it as teachable moment. He asked me what I thought as a Nigerian and I responded, "I do not know about that. Africa is a continent and not a country or village. My mother is the dominant person in my family. Without my mother, my father would not have been alive—she is the engine of my family. My father is very reserved and quite. I see that in many Nigerian families, specifically in many Ibo families." The professor asked the female student, "Who is the prime minister of India?" The student responded, "I don't really know. He must be one chauvinist pig." The professor turned to an Indian in the class and wanted to know what he thought; and he responded: "Indira Gandhi, a woman is the prime minister of India and she is very powerful not just in India but in the world. My mother is very strong and powerful. In fact, she runs my family and inspired me to pursue an advanced degree in the United States." Let us put this class situation in perspective! Indira Gandhi was the daughter of the first prime minister of India and later became the prime minister of India. She graduated from Visva-Bharati University in India, became a powerful world class politician. She served as prime minister of India for three terms (1966–1972) and was reelected for the fourth term in 1980 until she was assassinated on October 31, 1984.

Many changes are taking place today in our institutions, communities, states, nation, and world. The important question is, Are we ready to embrace these changes or do we want to remain static and retrogressively romanticize the yesteryears? In many nations of the world, we now have many female presidents and prime ministers who continue to make remarkable differences in the lives of others (read Richard O'Brien's 2017 book, *Women Presidents and Prime Ministers*). The world has had about 107 female leaders; and today in 2020, the United States of America is yet to elect its first female president. Going back to the story of my former classmate who was working on her PhD degree, she learned a lot from the class that she took with her immigrant classmates. What would have happened if the professor did not use the teachable moment constructively in our class? Many educational, social justice, and multicultural lessons would have been lost. This is why books like *Valuing Other Voices* are important to all, especially those who think that they know more than they know.

Let us dig deeper into my former classmate's chauvinistic assumptions about African men since I am a Nigerian American. The fact remains that her ill-informed or uninformed statement has many dangerous sociocultural, political, economic, and educational implications. In my interactions with colleagues, I have heard time and time again that African men are arrogant and chauvinistic, many a time without foundation. For example, I had a colleague at the University of Tennessee-Chattanooga who always told me to go to a speech and language pathologist privately and publicly to work on my accent even though I was always editing her manuscripts. Maybe in her mind she was caring; however, she did not understand the disastrous ramifications of her statement. One day, she wanted me to edit her manuscript that had series of editorial queries. In my response, I told her that I was on my way to a speech and language pathologist; and she got very irate. This same colleague started telling anyone who listened that I refused to edit her works because I was an arrogant chauvinist who had no respect for women. She forgot that I had edited for her more than 10 manuscripts that were accepted for publication. This was devastating to me—I could not defend myself since I was the only Black faculty in my department. As a teacher, scholar, and professional, I have found that whenever I refuse to take racist insults and humiliations, the "arrogance" label comes back to haunt me. And, as department head, I also found that many people tried to railroad me because I was a confident Black man from Nigeria. For instance, in the Ibo tribe, we hug a lot, greet people when we meet them, and appreciate their humanity. In the United States, I have learned to stop showing appreciation to individuals to avoid derogatory suppositions; yet on daily bases, men and women (including colleagues and students) compliment my taste in fashion and how I smell and dress. Even when I feel uncomfortable, I still thank them for valuing and appreciating my humanity.

Many multicultural lessons are exposed in *Valuing Other Voices*. For example, having an accent has nothing to do with one's ability to speak or write English well. It only shows an interference of mother tongue. That is why it hurts when one's accent affects his/her students' ratings in classes—these ratings frequently affect tenure and promotion decisions in colleges and universities. *It is absolutely critical to understand that a very simple negative assumption initiated by one misinformed or racist person can spread like wild fire and destroy a very thriving professional career.* Many distinguished professionals of African heritage have been hurt because of prejudicial assumptions; and they continue to endure hateful assumptions that have negatively affected their careers (Amman, 2002, 2003). Sadly, the underlying message in America seems to be that Africans and other minorities are sup-

xii *Valuing Other Voices*

posed to be seen and not heard—every day, we walk on egg shells in America's higher education. For example, in many departments and colleges/schools of education, people know the colleagues who are the "wolves;" however, nobody wants to confront them or be devoured by them. They are like gangs who conspire to attack and eliminate whoever challenges their supremacist or morally repugnant behaviors. Through the years, I have seen honorable people in higher education destroyed by this "herd mentality." Reading this book will help to reduce these extremely abusive, scary, sad, unfortunate, inhumane, and degrading behaviors at all educational levels.

In writing *Valuing Other Voices*, I wanted to touch on critical topics that have been vexing to many of us. We all know that when topics are vexing, they create unwarranted assumptions, illusory generalizations, and prejudicial conclusions. In addition, they lead to animus, hatred, and disunity in our communities, states, nations, and world. I believe it is important to discuss

- the multicultural fabric of education in the United States;
- the mythologies that hamper multicultural and global education;
- how "special" special education is for African Americans;
- leadership for changing times;
- how to go beyond silence in social justice and multiculturalism;
- the "model minority myth" and Asians in America's higher education;
- global learning and teaching in education;
- how to build self-concepts of vulnerable children and youth;
- the benefits of educating and hiring an "African" in America's higher education; and
- the "bandwagon effect" on thinking and society.

Hopefully, these discussions can lead to further discussions, related topics and discussions, and innovative solutions on our vexing problems.

Finally, I want people to read and think deeper about this book; and I want our actions to reflect our changing world. We need to open our doors to new ideas and talk more about them. Doing this book has been a rewarding experience for me—hopefully, you will find it rewarding to read. I thank Dr. Jacob Gordon for writing the foreword and Dr. Carol Huang for writing the afterword of this book. His perspective and voice have made my voice louder and reiterated the purpose of the book. I also thank the people at Information Age Publishing for believing in me and my voice. And, I especially thank my wife, Pauline Harris and children,

Charles Chidi, Gina Chioma, Kristen Ego, and Alicia Amaoge for their patience, love, blessing, and wisdom as I journey through life's complex mazes. To my friends, well-wishers, mentors, and mentees, you continue to enrich my life with all that you do to uplift humanity.

REFERENCES

Amman, M. (2002). Foreword: Blacks, Whites, and a cultural divide: Revelations of my American journey. In F. E. Obiakor & P. A. Grant (Eds.), *Foreign-born African Americans: Silenced voices in the discourse on race* (pp. xi–xvii). New York, NY: Nova Science.

Amman, M. (2003). And don't call me arrogant. In F. E. Obiakor & J. U. Gordon (Eds.), *African perspectives in American higher education: Invisible voices* (pp. 105–115). New York, NY: Nova Science.

King, C. S. (1983). *The words of Martin Luther King, Jr.* New York, NY: Newmarket Press.

O'Brien, R. (2017). *Women presidents and prime ministers: 2018 edition.* Washington, DC: Double Bridge.

CHAPTER 1

THE MULTICULTURAL FABRIC OF EDUCATION IN THE UNITED STATES

In Honor of "E Pluribus Unum"

Education has played major roles in advancing the multicultural fabric of the United States; and in turn, the United States has made efforts to challenge its schools and institutions to respond to current and future multicultural and global imperatives. It is no surprise that the missions, visions, strategic plans, and goals of schools and institutions continue to proactively address these imperatives. Without doubt, education continues to be viewed as a great and reliable equalizer in the American ways of living. Most human actions are centered in some sort of education; and education, in its broadest sense, is tied to culture, socioeconomics, politics, technology, and general ways of living (Beachum & Obiakor, 2018; Gibson & Obiakor, 2018; Obiakor, 2018).

It is critical that we recognize that our human valuing is much related to our human exposure or enlightenment; and our self-knowledge, self-esteem, and self-ideal are area specific based on our experiences. Interestingly, our experiences are perceived from differing lenses. We are all different; and we should be proud of our differences because they reflect who we are as human beings (Obiakor, 2001a, 2001b, 2008; Obiakor &

Valuing Other Voices: Discourses That Matter in Education, Social Justice, and Multiculturalism, pp. 1–5
Copyright © 2020 by Information Age Publishing
All rights of reproduction in any form reserved.

2 *Valuing Other Voices*

Martinez, 2018). Not only are people different intraindividually, they are also different interindividually. For example, in all innovative educational programs and teacher preparation programs, text books, theories, practices, curricula, major themes, and significant ideas focus on responding to individual differences. These differences manifest themselves in our intelligences, voices, likes, dislikes, abilities, disabilities, strengths, weaknesses, emotions, skin colors, personal idiosyncrasies, behaviors, learning styles, politics, socioeconomics, vulnerabilities, cultures, languages, values, national origins, genders, sexual orientations, religions, urban orientations, rural orientations, suburban orientations, to mention a few. In some ways, we are all vulnerable and different human beings; but, do we know that? Our generalizations, assumptions, perceptions, and prejudices are based on our jaundiced views; but, do we know that? Our efforts to silence other people's voices because they sound heretical do not mean that we should engage in heretical behaviors like silencing other people's voices; but, do we know that? For example, no intelligent human being will use "shithole" to describe countries and their peoples; but, do we know that? President Donald Trump of the United States, the leader of the greatest democracy in the world used "shithole" language in his immigration discussion in the White House.

"E PLURIBUS UNUM": **MEANING**

As a society, we continue to quantify human intelligences even though we know they are not good predictor variables of how successful we can be in the future. Yet, in some of our actions, some of us have continued to highlight our intellectual, cultural, or racial superiority or supremacy based on our differences. Funny enough, we acknowledge that we are different; but, in some strange fashion, we value our own unique differences better. Sadly, in most of our actions, we fail to honor our American motto: "*e pluribus unum*," the Latin for "out of many, one." *E pluribus unum* is alternatively translated as "one out of many" or "one from many." This motto was suggested by the Committee of Congress appointed on July 4, 1776, to design "a seal for the United States of America." Three times, the committee's recommendations failed. Later in 1782, Charles Thomson was selected to design the seal; and on June 30, 1782, he submitted his design to Congress—the great seal was approved on that same day.

The frantic efforts of our founding leaders demonstrate the respect that they have for the diversity of our nation. So, downplaying the spirits of our diversity is both ignorant and out of character. It is no surprise that in education, we challenge our students, teachers, leaders, and stakeholders to value and respect differences and diversities. In addition, we challenge our preservice teachers to have dispositions that are befitting of good teachers and practitioners. To a large measure, we challenge our teachers to identify, assess, label/categorize, place, and instruct our students and clients appropriately (Beachum & Obiakor, 2018; Gibson & Obiakor, 2018; Obiakor, 2018; Obiakor, Banks, Rotatori, & Utley, 2017). Even with all these challenges, our nation continues to be racialized; our societal equilibrium continues to be disrupted; and our politics, socioeconomics, and education continue to flounder in mediocrity. And, directly or indirectly, our general and special education programs continue to shamelessly misidentify, misassess, mislabel/miscategorize, misplace, and misinstruct our students (Obiakor, 2001a, 2001b). Simply put, valuing our differences has continued to haunt our general and special education establishments; and we continue to ask:

- Why do we still look at students and immediately make judgments about them before we get to know them even though we all agree that we are different and that "one cannot judge a book by its cover"?
- While do we still use instruments that have been proven to lack reliability and validity to assess our students even though we know that these scores are not good predictor variables of how intelligent or successful someone can be?
- Why do we still label or categorize our students based on results from unreliable and valid tools even though we know the devastating consequences of labels and categories?
- Why do we still place our students in restrictive settings of education based on their labels even though we know that disproportionate placements destroy the spirits of inclusive education or education in general?
- Why do we still recklessly teach students without recognizing their styles, strengths, and weaknesses even though we know that human beings are different and instructional differentiation is the engine of effective learning and teaching?
- Why do we still do so many evil things that harm our students and impede their learning even though we know that these harmful things will force them to hate school and drop out of school?
- Why do we still suspend and expel our students from school even though we know that they set up our students for the criminal and prison pipelines?
- Why do we still pretend that we do not know what to do with our students even though we know exemplary programs that will enhance their success rates in school and in life?

MOVING FORWARD

Looking at the aforementioned questions, one will think that we are at the end of the road. In his frustration and quest for racial justice, Bell (1985, 1992) alluded to the permanence of racism. From my perspective, he was both right and wrong. Yes, our struggles for diversity seem insurmountable; however, we cannot in good conscience fold our tents and disappear into the woods. That, in itself, is what makes the United States the greatest country in the world. Our struggles frequently fortify our resilience, resolve, and positive actions.

In education, we seem to be moving forward despite our traditional burdens. For example, in some school districts, innovative programs have been designed to close achievement gaps at some levels. But, we need innovative leaders and change agents who are willing to take risks and do what is right to build bridges and programs that have proven to be effective in maximizing the fullest potential of learners and teachers (Obiakor et al., 2017). The educational politics of yesterday has been destructive and fruitless—it has created divisions that have hampered collaboration, consultation, and cooperation at different levels. We do not have to reinvent the wheel, so to say! We now know what works; and it is time we started replicating what works. Moving forward, in education and other related professions, we must come to some operational human thinking that should guide our "modus vivendi," namely:

- Human beings are different.
- Differences are not deficits.
- Culture is an integral part of life.
- There is no "shithole" race, country, or people.
- Bad educators and leaders silence "new" and different voices.
- All Whites are not racist, bigoted, or xenophobic.
- Blacks, Latinos, Native Americans, or Asians can be racist, bigoted, or xenophobic.
- Whites can be lazy.
- Blacks, Latinos, Native Americans, or Asians can be lazy.
- A "rich" person can be morally bankrupt.
- Poverty does not mean "poor" morals or "poor" zest for life's success.
- Blacks, Latinos, Native Americans, or Asians can be more intelligent than Whites, and vice versa.
- All Asians are not "model" minorities.

- The world is full of "good" and "bad" people; but, it has more good people than bad people.
- Linguistic colonialism diminishes the valuing of mother tongue (i.e., native language).
- Racism, religious bigotry, and xenophobia are not over in the United States.
- All Muslims are not terrorists.
- All Christians are not nice people.
- If we do not change as people, we will be consumed by change.
- We must be vigilant about our future as a community of peoples.
- What we put into our community is what we get.

CONCLUSION

"E pluribus unum" is the motto of the United States; and we need to take it seriously. It defines what our country is all about; yet it has not been given its due attention by many of our citizens. It not only exposes our diversity as a nation, it also cherishes the diversity of our opinions and values. Our educational leaders and even our sociopolitical leaders have not put the proper spirit of our motto into full practical perspectives. It is imperative that our deliberations, dealings, and actions have diversity as the engine that drives them. We can no longer afford to live with the falsity that our diversity is socially manufactured or miraculously engineered. Our diversity is our root—it transcends our livelihood as a multicultural people with diversified views, *one* purpose, and *one* nation. Even though minority voices are silenced in some quarters, we refuse to be invisible people (Ellison, 1952; Obiakor, 2018; Obiakor & Martinez, 2018). Our schools, institutions, colleges, and universities must reflect our diversities; and our educators and teacher preparation programs must require multicultural infusion as a powerful part of our activities in student, faculty, staff, and leadership recruitment, retention, tenure, and promotion. Again, we do not have to reinvent the wheels—we know what works; and we just need to do what works in our teaching and learning processes.

CHAPTER 2

ADDRESSING MYTHOLOGIES THAT HAMPER MULTICULTURAL AND GLOBAL EDUCATION

More than 8 decades ago, Gertrude Stein (1937), in her book, *Everybody's Autobiography*, coined the famous quote, "There is no there there." Literally, this statement can be interpreted to mean that there is no veracity or truthfulness to an issue or a topic. However, in life, sometimes, there is a there there, if we look hard enough. And, in today's sociopolitical climate in the United States, we have been bombarded with myriad mythologies, presumptions, and suppositions that have produced illusory generalizations about one situation or another. It is no surprise that we now have phrases like "fake news" or what President Trump's former campaign manager and current counselor, Kellyanne Conway (2017) called, "alternative facts." While mythologies are not new to our respective communities, they have exploded in very harmful and damaging ways in the United States. For instance, consider the fact that the dictators and spies of socialist Russia took advantage of these mythologies to meddle in our democratic 2016 Presidential elections to favor one candidate over another. As a result, inquisitive minds are rightly intrigued to ask, "Is there a there there with regard to these mythologies?"

Of late, many citizens in the United States have been myopically enthused by some strange feel-good mythologies like *"we must take our country back," "we must make America great again," "we must make America safe again," "North Atlantic Treaty Organization is obsolete," "we must exit the Paris*

Valuing Other Voices: Discourses That Matter in Education, Social Justice, and Multiculturalism, pp. 7–13
Copyright © 2020 by Information Age Publishing
All rights of reproduction in any form reserved.

7

8 *Valuing Other Voices*

Climate Accord," "we can longer appease or apologize to the world," "we can no longer allow refugees from certain Muslim nations to come into the United States," "countries should pay for their own military defense," "immigrants are draining our economy so let's not let them in," "Muslims are Islamic terrorists who should not be allowed into our country," "we will build a wall and Mexico will pay for it," Former President Obama is a foreign born from Kenya who came to rule the United States out of nowhere, to mention a few. People have rationalized these feel-good mythological statements because they seem to make them proud to be Americans and show America's indispensability to the rest of the world. However, they have far-reaching consequences to the magnanimous image of our great country. First, they portray us to be ignorant, danger-ous, hateful, nativist, provincial, bigoted, White supremacist, xenophobic, presumptuous, racist, insensitive, and close minded. Second, they perpet-uate negative labels, racist perceptions, prejudicial stereotypes, dehuman-izing categories, and illusory generalizations of fellow humans. Third, they lead to hateful deadly attacks on innocent citizens who have done nothing to hurt us. Fourth, they fail to show us as a great democratic country that has been prudent in the ways it has collaborated, consulted, and cooperated with other nations. And fifth, they downplay the reality that our world will not be our world today without multicultural and global understanding, appreciation, and education.

As a very responsible and productive citizen of the United States, I proudly believe in "America first" and also believe we are the greatest country in the world. My belief is, however, not based on our military might, racist arrogance, or xenophobia—it is based on the goodness of America and the strength of America as the greatest democracy in the world. I am proud of what America has done for me; and I see nothing wrong with the self-pride that is based on the role of the United States in building, sustaining, and developing humanity. For example, I value our roles in helping to sustain the United Nations, Worldwide Hunger Relief, Inc., World Health Organization, United Nations Educational, Scientific, and Cultural Organization, United Nations International Children Edu-cation Fund, World Bank, Doctors Without Borders, International Mone-tary Fund, World Trade Organization, International Atomic Energy Agency, Amnesty International, Friends of the Earth International, World Wildlife Fund for Nature, North Atlantic Treaty Organization, Green-peace, to mention a few. The United States continues to demonstrate its remarkable goodness in working with refugees who are stranded and dev-astated by wars all over the world. And, the United States continues to help our world citizens who have suffered from disruptions, disasters, and deaths (Obiakor, Mehring, & Schwenn, 1997). Simply put, I cherish the marks of our greatness as a country in supporting our global village.

Addressing Mythologies That Hamper Multicultural and Global Education 9

BEYOND TRADITIONAL MYTHOLOGIES

It is critical that the citizens of the United States respond to the mythologies that continue to hamper our multicultural and global understanding and valuing. I acknowledge my naïveté in thinking that my simple explanations will eliminate long lasting mythologies and assumptions. However, not trying to explain or respond to them is a great danger to our democracy and a great miseducation about our cultures and our world. While I fundamentally believe in the greatness of the United States, I believe our own arrogance as a people has been counterproductive to how we are perceived by other peoples of the world. Consider a few responses to these traditional mythologies that have caused more problems than they can ever solve. For example, when we talk about "taking our country back," we forget that we are a country of immigrants. It is an historical fact that Native Americans are original settlers of our country. When we talk about "making America great again," we fail to acknowledge that America has been and will continue to be the greatest country in the world by most measurable standards. It is no surprise that it is still the dream country of many citizens of the world because of the multidimensional opportunities that are available here. When we talk about "making America safe again," the question is, compared with where? In African nations, there are unending tribal and religious wars. In the Middle East, there are unending divisional, religious, and terrorist fears. In Eastern and Western Europe, there are unending struggles between capitalism and communism and unending fears of terrorism because of their geographical locations. In Asiatic nations, there are perpetual multidimensional struggles that threaten their sacred existence. Because of America's democracy and religious freedom, people are freer to worship than in most parts of the world. When we talk about the North Atlantic Treaty Organization being obsolete, we forget the support from the North Atlantic Treaty Organization in defeating communism and in fighting terrorist organizations like the Taliban after the September 11, 2001 terrorist attack in our country.

On the issue of reneging on the Paris, France climate accord, the United States will lose its footing as a global leader in matters of importance. What makes us great as a nation is our ability to lead on humanity-related issues to uplift our globe. For example, nothing prevents us from leading on new energy initiatives! In addition, it is politically and economically savvy for us to apologize for our past mistakes as needed! It is pretty arrogant and uncooperative to believe we are always right while others are always wrong. It puts our citizens in precarious positions when we selfishly impose our wills on others without recognizing the self-determination of other nations. It is presumptuous to think that we are supe-

10 *Valuing Other Voices*

rior in everything that we do. Does this arrogance not force other countries to do whatever they can to prove us wrong? In today's dangerous world where people have many diabolic means to prove themselves, it is not a very good omen for our citizens who are simply trying to maximize their fullest potential in their respective lives and businesses. On the issue of countries paying for their military defense, it sounds very naively attractive. The danger there is that countries will be hesitant to support us when we are in wars ourselves. As the old African proverb goes, "you cannot climb a tree without support."

On issues of immigrants draining our economy and not letting them into the United States, the simple answer is that we are a nation of immigrants. Many of our inventions in technology and education are results of contributions from generations of immigrants. Simply put, without immigrants, our nation will not be measurably great! On issues of building a wall and making Mexico to pay for it, it is silly, intolerant, hateful, xenophobic, and unrealistic. Our goal as a nation should be to destroy boundaries and barriers and create opportunities for more interactions and discourses among peoples. Finally, the worst of all the mythologies in the United States is the denial of former President Obama's rights as a citizen. The Birther Movement led by President Donald Trump has been a cheap political ploy to delegitimize former President Obama and deny him as a citizen of the United States—clearly, this movement has been extremely racist, shamefully disgraceful, and grossly ignorant. The reality is that the former president was born in the United States and raised by his White grandparents and White mother from Kansas.

I can go on and on in addressing the dangers of our traditional mythologies. Sadly, these mythologies have magnified the illusions of what we think we are to the world, where we are as a leader in the world, and where we think we are going in this complex world. In addition, these mythologies have created boundaries, fears, and deadly hateful crimes that have become cancerous cells eating deeper into our very soul as a nation. These abnormalities might be good ploys to win elections, but they are having devastating effects in building our confidence as the greatest nation in the world. This is the more reason why we must expand the pace of multicultural and global education in our classrooms, schools, colleges/universities, communities, states, nations, and world (Obiakor, 2017). We can no longer afford to be fraudulent multiculturalists and closet xenophobes who are divorced from global or life's realities; and we can no longer continue to pretend that there is no there there, especially following the devastating effects of unconscionable mythologies in the United States.

WHAT EDUCATORS AND LEADERS
CAN DO TO SEE THE THERE THERE

Educators and leaders have roles to play in challenging existing hateful mythologies and in debunking negative assumptions about the world in which we live. When it comes to xenophobia, racism, ethnocentrism, and other close-minded behaviors in the United States, we must continue to ask the question, Is there a there, there? Based on my answers to the aforementioned mythologies, one can conclude that "there is a there there." But, to see the there there, it is critical that we see beyond our eyes, look hard enough, and search for the truth to discover our confusions, disconnections, and disruptions. Yes, we are "a nation divided and afraid" today because we have planted the poisonous seeds of hate and created the xenophobic climate that discourages multicultural and global understanding, appreciation, and education. It behooves us as citizens, students, educators, scholars, community leaders, and political leaders to understand how we have created illusions and mythologies that have measurably hampered (and will continue to hamper) our ability to grow as human beings and as a nation.

As indicated, educators and leaders have roles to play in building our global village. Rather than create boundaries and fears for cheap political gains, we must see the world as a place where we must get along as a village. Valuing our global village must entail frantic efforts to:

- solidify existing worldwide alliances and organizations;
- collaborate in sociocultural missions with other countries;
- expand international games such as the Olympics, Para-Olympics, World Cup Soccer, X Games, Summer Games, Winter Games, to mention a few;
- increase international trades and relations to build global economies;
- expand economic, social, educational, and political interactions to buttress mutual respect;
- improve democratic ideas and ideals throughout the world;
- make gender equality a priority in developed and developing countries;
- improve literacy at all levels of nation building in even the remotest areas of the world;
- reduce religious boundaries at community, national, and global levels; and

12 *Valuing Other Voices*

- bridge gaps between the "rich" and the "poor" to improve healthy living standards at all global levels.

Specifically, educators and leaders in the United States must begin to recreate and redesign educational programs from prekindergarten to university levels to advance the principles of collaboration, consultation, and cooperation. Special attention must be paid to funding innovative programs that highlight the comprehensive support model, a model that takes advantage of the collaborative energies of students, educational professionals, parents, community leaders, and government agencies. Interestingly, the Council for the Accreditation of Educator Preparation (2013) recognized the roles of diversity, technology, and partnerships in making programmatic advancements. We must understand that we live in a diverse world and in a technologically improving era that makes the world smaller and smaller. Such an understanding will buttress our partnerships at different educational, economic, social, community, national, and global levels. We must take advantage of national and international conventions and conferences that bring together growing students and innovative educators, researchers, and scholars for the common good. We must continue to advance international programs, study abroad programs, and exchange programs among students, educators, and leaders to expose people to the beauties of other nations. Finally, we must continue to search for the unending truth to debunk mythologies. Of what use is education if it does not increase discourses and relationships at all levels? We can no longer afford to live in fears unsubstantiated presumptions. We must refocus and redesign programs that foster global unity at classroom, school, college, and university levels. And, we must build entities that enhance our unity of purpose as a global village. In the end, we must light the candles in others instead of cursing the darkness in them.

CONCLUSION

It is evident that multicultural and global understanding, appreciation, and education are necessary to build harmony, unity, and advancements at all levels. We live in dangerous times when mythologies and presumptions dominate our discourses and create more complex problems for our world. In the United States, these assumptions have stolen the souls of some of our citizens and made some of us zombies without critical thinking skills. To a large measure, our greatness as a nation is now under fire! We are losing our respect as the greatest democracy in the world—we are beginning to lose our moral authority in telling other countries what to

Addressing Mythologies That Hamper Multicultural and Global Education 13

do to improve themselves economically, socially, politically, and educationally.

Clearly, there is a there there, especially if one analyzes the current state of affairs in the United States! No civilized country can ever sustain itself with the myriad mythologies that are floating around its existence as a country. Retreating from the world's stage, isolating ourselves from the rest of the world, and divorcing ourselves from the realities of life will only reduce the power of the United States as a leader of the free world. We must go beyond mythologies to build bridges that enhance socioeconomic, political, and peaceful relationships at worldwide levels. There are already organizations in place to build global bridges—we must make frantic efforts to solidify existing entities and programs. Engaging in racist, xenophobic, White supremacist and ethnocentric miseducation that forces us to retreat back into our individual cocoons will only exacerbate our global problems. We appear to be angrier, more hateful, and less welcoming of international ideas and ideals that have reinforced our strength as a global leader. Finally, we need serious educational, economic, political, religious, and social leaders to proactively involve themselves in innovative programs that can measurably foster global collaboration, consultation, and cooperation. There must be concerted efforts to bring different leaders from different countries together to solidify global initiatives and create new unifying avenues for peace and prosperity at all global levels. We are now civilized and sophisticated enough to avoid global conflicts that could result in another world war—all hands must finally be on deck!

CHAPTER 3

HOW "SPECIAL" IS SPECIAL EDUCATION FOR AFRICAN AMERICANS IN THE UNITED STATES?

As an African American, I have often wondered why the majority of students placed in special education programs come from culturally and linguistically diverse (CLD) backgrounds. And, I continue to wonder why nothing is done to remediate this situation. My simple answer is that people expect it to be that way. If not, why does it not seriously bother or shame general and special educators, school leaders, community leaders, and government agencies that a group of individuals in our society is misidentified, misassessed, mislabeled, misplaced, and misinstructed? Interestingly, this "business-as-usual" mentality continues to prevail even though special education is an important educational phenomenon that is supposed to help all children and youth with special needs to maximize their fullest potential (Blackhurst & Berdine, 1993; Obiakor, Utley, & Rotatori, 2003; Smith & Tyler, 2010). According to Blackhurst and Berdine (1993), special education ought to provide services different from, supplementary with, and additional to those provided in a regular classroom with a systematic modification and adaptation of instruction, equipment, and materials.

Based on the above definition, special education is a much needed service for all children and youth struggling to succeed in academic arenas. In other words, at-risk, disadvantaged, disenfranchised, urban, suburban,

Valuing Other Voices: Discourses That Matter in Education, Social Justice, and Multiculturalism, pp. 15–27

Copyright © 2020 by Information Age Publishing
All rights of reproduction in any form reserved.

15

16 *Valuing Other Voices*

rural, poor, homeless, and CLD students would benefit from special education. As it appears for many African Americans, the reverse tends to be the case. Rather than remediate their problems, special education tends to upgrade and perpetuate their problems. It is no wonder that these students continue to endure problems and crisis in today's general and special education programs. The question then is, what can we do about these problems? In this chapter, I respond to the question by sharing my perspective on special education in the United States.

HISTORICAL CONTEXTS AND REALITIES

From time immemorial, individuals with special needs have lived in our midst. They have existed, functioned, and participated in our societal functions in one way or another. For instance, the Jewish Talmud, Moslem Koran, and Christian Bible made particular references to persons with special needs. In fact, all societies, including the United States have continued to focus on how to take care of their less fortunate, less powerful, disenfranchised, and disadvantaged (Obiakor & Algozzine, 1995a). Since racism and classism have become an integral part of the United States' society, African Americans fall under this less fortunate, less powerful, disenfranchised, and disadvantaged group. And, for African Americans with special needs, their problems become doubly troublesome. From these historical contexts, it appears that efforts have concentrated on how to tolerate and/or victimize African Americans with special needs rather than on functional goal-directed efforts to truly educate them with *real pedagogical power*. Earlier, Hillard (1992) observed that real pedagogical power means that "all children who may have disabilities receive sophisticated, valid services that cause them to do better than they would have done if they had not received special services at all" (p. 168).

In the late 18th century, Jean Marc Itard, a French physician believed in real pedagogical power when he decided to take on the task of educating Victor, the "wild boy" of Aveyron, France. Even this wild boy was able to acquire some skills, an indication that special education works when done right. In the early parts of the 20th century, Dr. Alfred Binet, the brain behind the current Stanford-Binet Intelligence Scale, noted that human knowledge and/or intelligence can be improved. Using his experiences with his special class, Binet (1909) warned against the over reliance on his intelligence quotient tool. As he remarked, "It is in this parochial sense, the only one accessible to us, that we say that intelligence of these children has been increased. We have increased what constitutes the intelligence of a pupil: the capacity to learn and to assimilate instruction" (p.104). A logical extension is that no brain is a tabula rasa (blank slate); in other words, all children can learn. Two critical questions come to mind

How "Special" Is Special Education for African Americans in the United States? 17

at this juncture. Why is it that today's special education does not help to improve the intelligence of African Americans placed in it? And, why is it that bright African American students are devalued and inappropriately placed in special education programs? More than three decades ago, Gould (1981) decried the mismeasure of persons and argued that "if Binet's principles had been followed, and his tests consistently used as he intended, we would have been spared a major misuse of science in our century" (p. 155). In addition, he warned against the blind following of the theory of biological determinism (i.e., the belief that human attributes are only genetically based) because it hampers human valuing and the ability to engage in real pedagogical power. Goodlad (1993) corroborated Gould's premise and noted that:

> We appear incapable of getting beyond individuals as the units of assessment with the accompanying allocation of responsibility for success and failure. We must adopt as standard practice the kind of contextual appraisal that tells whether schools have in place the curriculum, materials, pedagogy, and other conditions necessary to the good education of individuals. The absence of these exposes and brings inequities that are the moral responsibility of a caring people in a just society to correct. (p. 20)

There is no doubt that African American students with special needs deserve to be educated. The question is, Why do we frequently forget the broad goals of special education when we deal with African American learners? I wonder why the goals for educating these learners are not in alliance with the goals of special education. Like other groups in the United States, African Americans have people with special needs. As a matter of fact, we have African Americans with cognitive disabilities, learning disabilities, emotional/behavioral disorders, communication disorders/speech and language impairments, visual impairment/blindness, hearing impairment/deafness, autism, traumatic brain injury, gifted and talented, physical disabilities, and other health impairments. While there are more African Americans in some categories than others, they all deserve to maximize their fullest potential in life. The major problem, however, is that rather than help them to maximize their potential, special education as a process has sadly led to their misidentification, misassessment, miscategorization, misplacement, and misinstruction (Obiakor, 2001, 2004, 2007; Obiakor et al., 2004; Obiakor & Ford, 2002; Utley & Obiakor, 2001).

IN SEARCH OF EQUITY

It is a natural instinct for people to associate with those who behave, look, speak, and act like them. Anyone who does not fall in that norm is traditionally misperceived, mistreated, and miseducated (James, 1958;

18 *Valuing Other Voices*

Obiakor, 2008, 2009). Since African Americans do not fit into the norm, it should be no surprise that those with special needs have been discriminated against, ostracized, labeled, and called demeaning names (e.g., stupid and retarded). Today, advocates of these students have pressed for ways to positively respond to their unique needs in quantifiable ways (Obiakor, Harris, & Beachum, 2009).

In the United States, it is impossible to divorce the education of African American students from the Civil Rights Movement and the subsequent events that followed. To a great extent, the education of these students has been historically influenced by social developments and court decisions in the 1950s and 1960s. For example, the landmark *Brown v. Board of Education of Topeka* (1954) case was a civil rights case that declared separate education as unequal education and unconstitutional (Obiakor, 2009). This was significant because it had the goal of ending racial segregation in schools. The ruling of this case became a catalyst that prompted parents and professionals to lobby for equitable education for their students. The *Brown* ruling led to more landmark cases that have had historical and educational impacts. For example, the *Pennsylvania Association for Retarded Children v. Commonwealth of Pennsylvania* (1972) case held that children could not be denied access to public schools, and entitled them to a free and appropriate public education. In the *Mills v. Board of Education* (1972) case, a class action lawsuit was filed on behalf of 18,000 children with varied special needs in the Washington, DC schools. In this case, the court ordered the district to educate all children with special needs and further clarified that specific procedures had to be followed to determine whether a student should receive special services. Generally, these cases and other subsequent cases formed the framework for the laws that currently guide the field of special education (Yell, 2004). The question is, What have we learned from these court cases regarding the education of African Americans with special needs?

In consonance, many laws have historically impacted the fields of general and special education. For instance, the 1964 Civil Rights Act (PL 88-352) provided legal rights to equality in education and other sectors of human interactions. In 1973, Section 504 of the Vocational Rehabilitation Act (PL 93-112) was passed to provide persons with special needs with (a) free and appropriate public education, (b) civil rights, (c) accessibility of programs, and (d) employability rights. In 1975, the Education of All Handicapped Children's Act (PL 94-142) was passed with the following fundamental ingredients: (a) education for students from 3-21 years, (b) free and appropriate public education, (c) identification of students, (d) nondiscriminatory assessments, (e) placement in the least restrictive environment, (f) confidentiality of information, (g) procedural safeguards, and (h) development of individualized education plans. In 1986, PL 94-

How "Special" Is Special Education for African Americans in the United States? 19

142 was amended to accommodate young children from birth to 3 years. This law (PL 99-457) was enacted to provide not just individualized education plans for children but also individual family support programs for parents and guardians. In 1990, PL 94-142 was renamed as the Individuals with Disabilities Education Act (IDEA; PL 101-476). This Act involved funding for states to provide educational services to students from birth through 21, and ensured procedural safeguards for parents that guarantee meaningful participation in the evaluation process (Katisyannis, Yell, & Bradley, 2001). Additionally, IDEA guaranteed improvement in the education of students with special needs through research training, technical supports, and transitional supports for students. To challenge the private sectors, the 1990 American with Disabilities Act (PL 101-336) was passed to provide more societal opportunities for persons with special needs. In 1997, IDEA was reauthorized as PL 105-17 to facilitate disciplinary procedures and reduce litigation costs. In 2001, the No Child Left Behind Act (PL 107-110) was passed to educate all learners and quantifiably account for their progress at all levels. Later, in 2004, IDEA was again reauthorized as the Individuals with Disabilities Education Improvement Act (PL 108-446). This law mandated that teachers of students with special needs be highly qualified, meaning they must be certified in the content areas that they are teaching (T. E. Smith, 2005). Not long ago, a new law (Pub. L. 114-95), Every Child Succeeds Act was passed on December 10, 2015, to reauthorize the 1965 Elementary and Secondary Education Act. While these governmental efforts are laudable, the questions continue to be, What impacts have these laws had in the education of African Americans with special needs? And, why do African American students still endure disproportionate placements in special education?

CONTEMPORARY CHALLENGES AND PROSPECTS

The goal of any educational program is to maximize the fullest potential of its students. In the same vein, the goal must be to truly leave no African American child behind despite his/her ability or disability. The critical question remains, Do we stay the course, resist change, or move forward in the education of African American students with special needs? More than a decade ago, Schrag (1993) confirmed that "the proportion of students being served within special education programs today and in the future is changing, which requires closer integration and coordination of services within the educational system and with a broader array of health and social services" (p. 208). The response of the federal government with regard to these imperatives has been "accountability without accountability" (i.e., accountability that focuses narrowly on the exclusion of African

20   *Valuing Other Voices*

American students via traditional assessments). Sadly, some accountability measures are already hurting the spirit of special education for students who need it. In his piece titled, "The Death of Special Education," Lieberman (2001) argued that:

> Special education has been swallowed by the beast: the school system, with its mandated curriculum, mandated tests, and mandated standards. Now, children with disabilities are entitled—no, are practically required—to have the same education as every other child, regardless of whether or not that education is of high quality or is appropriate for a child with a disability. (p. 39)

While it is iconoclastic to believe special education "has been swallowed by the beast" because of accountability challenges that are forced upon it, it is equally unrealistic to assume that we should just "stay the course" in special education. Any field or profession that does not believe in positive change is dead. Clearly, recent demographic changes in our society have challenged general and special educators and leaders to look for innovative ways to maximize the potential of all their students, including African Americans (Obiakor, 2007; Rueda, 2007). As Rueda (2007) argued, "given the longstanding but continuing controversy over the issue of overrepresentation of diverse students in special education, the future implications for identification, referral, assessment, and instructions are abundant" (p. 292). To maximize the fullest potential of African Americans with special needs, general and special educators must respond to contemporary realities, avoid historical mistakes, and advance the field of special education. In a more targeted fashion, they must make efforts to (a) go beyond tradition to listen to new voices in the field, and (b) shift paradigms in educator/professional preparation.

Listening to New Voices in the Field

Of late, there have been some traditional moves to silence new voices and/or critics of the current system of special education even though this current system tends to over represent CLD students (in this case, African American learners) in programs for children with emotional/behavioral disorders and underrepresent them in programs for students with gifts and talents. Kauffman (2002, 2003a, 2003b, 2004); Mostert, Kauffman, and Kavale (2003); and Sasso (2003) have been critical of these new voices. As these scholars noted, it is wrong to criticize the current system of special education because such criticisms are anti-special education. In fact, in their works, they have been less receptive to the fact that the disproportionate representation of CLD students (in this case,

How "Special" Is Special Education for African Americans in the United States? 21

African American learners) is actually not good for special education. For instance, Kauffman (2003b) argued that:

> The assumption that special education, which is at its best the fair treatment of disability, *creates* stigma is not just wrong; it is perverse. It confuses treatment with cause, just as if we were to make the assumption that identifying and treating cancer caused the stigma that used to accompany having it. Without willingness to talk about disabilities in a simple and straightforward way, we cannot address the problem of stigma. Euphemisms are cloaks that hide nothing effectively. Always and inevitably, they are stumbling rags that trip up prevention. (p. 196)

There is some truth that the current special education system may work for some African American children and youth. However, the question is, Do we as critics of the current special education system for African Americans believe in the spirit of special education? Sure, we do! I believe special education works well when it does not misidentify, misassess, miscategorize, misplace, and misinstruct African American students because they are racially, culturally, linguistically, and socioeconomically different. It seems unprofessional and immoral to hide under the cloak of special education to get rid of African American students in school programs just because they exhibit different behavioral and learning styles. Again, while there is great need for evidence-based practice in special education, I strongly disagree with Kauffman's (2003a) assertion that "if you discount science as a way of finding things out and believe that special education is fundamentally flawed, second rate, ineffective, unfair, and oppressive, then you're not going to use it for prevention" (p. 206). It is my fundamental belief that science is necessary; however, the indiscriminate use of a scientifically proven medication to cure all illnesses is dangerous, unethical, and immoral (Obiakor, 2004). The "heart" or respect for humanity must be incorporated into whatever we do as professionals even though one's "heart" or spirituality cannot be measured. Science may not always be the only answer in special education; feelings should matter too! Even in the medical field, the touch of the doctor and the feelings of the patient can facilitate and advance the healing process. Why should the education of African American students with exceptionalities be any different?

In their study titled, "Do race of student and race of teacher influence ratings of emotional and behavioral problem characteristics of students with emotional disturbance?", Cullinan and Kauffman (2005) concluded that "results did not support the position that, among students with ED [emotional disturbance], overrepresentation of African Americans arises from racial bias in teacher perceptions of emotional and behavioral problems" (p. 393). Coupled with the study's limitations and weaknesses as identified by Cullinan and Kauffman, there is the presumption of inno-

22 *Valuing Other Voices*

cence of teachers just because of their race or culture. In many urban schools in this United States, there are African American educators, leaders, and professionals who through their actions have devastated the lives of African American students and their parents (Obiakor, 2001b, 2003). In addition, historically, have we not seen some African American policemen or women who have wrongfully arrested, brutalized, shot, and killed fellow African Americans in strange attempts to maintain law and order (Prater, 2006)? Their race or culture must never be an alibi that exonerates them from being criticized or sued for violating the civil rights of others. Furthermore, have we not seen a poorly prepared African American educator or service provider who has been professionally devastating to African American students (Obiakor, 1999, 2001b, 2003, 2004, 2007, 2008, 2009; Obiakor & Beachum, 2005; Obiakor & Ford, 2002; Obiakor, Grant, & Dooley, 2002; Utley & Obiakor, 2001)? In my view, a good educator or practitioner is a good professional, despite his race, language, culture, or national origin.

We need new voices to advance the historical importance of special education. I believe the whole process of special education must be appropriate for all students, including African American students with special needs. It is imperative that general and special educators and leaders demonstrate their willingness to listen to new voices in the African American community by:

- developing and using identification, assessment, and instructional strategies that function within the context of cultural competence;
- creating a collaborative system of community support that focuses on eradicating social stereotyping based on race, ethnicity, national origin, gender, and socioeconomic status;
- developing an awareness and appreciation for the many family forms that value individual differences and strengths;
- thwarting conditions that lead to violence in the home or community and cultivate a sense of safety for children and families;
- advocating economic policies and human services that are profamily by virtue of proven outcomes;
- promoting culturally competent practices in schools and in the larger society to respect differences in worldviews and learning styles among individuals;
- advocating expanded services that provide for affordable quality childcare to meet the varied needs of all families and children;
- developing collaborative community approaches to problem solving that involve students, parents, schools, and community leaders;

How "Special" Is Special Education for African Americans in the United States?   23

- recognizing that the focus of the problem in at-risk situations is not only in the individual but also in institutional barriers in the environment;
- reconfiguring curricula that incorporate culturally sensitive variables;
- reinstituting rites of passage and service opportunities that cultivate a sense of belonging and resiliency in youth; and
- broadening visions in educational reform that include economic reform and the investment in human capital.

Apparently, by listening to new voices, general and special educators can assist African American students in maximizing their potential in school programs. For instance, they can prevent and manage violent behaviors that have created psychological setbacks for their students by shifting their own personal paradigms. In contrast to the "get-tough" no-nonsense approaches (e.g., zero tolerance or three-strikes-you-are-out disciplinary models), school personnel can teach prosocial skills and educate their African American students to manage interpersonal conflicts nonviolently (Goldstein, 1999; Long, 1997; Obiakor, 2001a). After a lifetime of experience with youth with emotional/behavioral disorders, Long (1997) simply suggested using "kindness" or what we call the "heart" in dealing with students. General and special educators employing caring transitional strategies for African American students must focus on a variety of communication skills that enable young people to manage their behaviors and respond to others in ways that do not provoke confrontations. Educators must revisit the traditional emphasis on intelligence or academic achievement that seems to downplay the emotional intelligence and resiliency needed to survive in a changing society (Gardner, 1993; Goleman, 1995; Obiakor, Enwefa, Utley, Obi, Gwalla-Ogisi, & Enwefa, 2004; Obiakor, Mehring, & Schwenn, 1997). As Goleman (1995) remarked, emotional intelligence entails "abilities such as being able to motivate oneself and persist in the face of frustrations; to control impulse and delay gratification; to regulate one's moods and keep distress from swamping the ability to think; to empathize and to hope" (p. 34). He added:

> Academic intelligence offers virtually no preparation for the turmoil—or opportunity—life's vicissitudes bring. Yet even though a high IQ is no guarantee of prosperity, prestige, or happiness in life, our schools and our culture fixate on academic abilities, ignoring emotional intelligence, a set of traits—some might call it character—that also matters immensely for our personal destiny. (p. 36)

We need new voices to advance proactive measures that have been found to foster emotional intelligence in African American learners,

24 *Valuing Other Voices*

including those with special needs. These measures must incorporate partnership programs, prosocial skills instructional programs, and mentorship programs. How can African American students value differences if differences are not valued in their homes, schools, and communities? How can they work together if adults and communities fail to work together? People who have emotional intelligence can help dissipate some of the cultural forms of "heartlessness" that permeate schools, for example, put-downs based upon race, ethnicity, gender, or disability. African American students must learn to work together, their families must learn to cooperate with each other, and their schools must learn to work collaboratively with their communities (Obiakor et al., 2002; Obiakor et al., 2004). These collaborative and consultative behaviors frequently lead to cooperative resolutions of conflict and help African American students, parents, and professionals to maximize their potential.

Shifting Paradigms in Educator/Professional Preparation Programs

Like all students, African American students exhibit different learning and behavioral patterns. But for some reason, these students are intentionally or unintentionally misidentified, misassessed, miscategorized, misplaced, and misinstructed in school programs (Mukuria & Obiakor, 2004; Obiakor, 1999, 2001b, 2003, 2007; Obiakor & Beachum, 2005; Obiakor & Wilder, 2003; Utley & Obiakor, 2001). What then are the roles of professional preparation programs for African American learners? Even with the best intentions, many colleges and universities have failed to satisfactorily prepare educators for today's classrooms. Earlier, Haberman (1995) asserted that upon completion of traditional teaching programs teachers and service providers are as prepared for today's classrooms as a swimmer who prepared for the English Channel by training in the university swimming pool. It is important that teacher educators and leaders take the bull by its horns! They must be professionally responsible—they must prepare general and special educators and leaders to respond to demographic changes. In addition, they must shift their own paradigms to prepare teachers and leaders who will shift their own paradigms (Smith, Richards, MacGrawley, & Obiakor, 2001; Winzer & Mazurek, 1998).

For general and special education professionals engaged in research, they must broaden their horizons in their understanding of the African American nature and nurture and other human behaviors and attributes. As scholars, educational professionals must go beyond the archaic theory of biological determinism and the myth of socioeconomic dissonance to

How "Special" Is Special Education for African Americans in the United States? 25

make sense of their research (Gould, 1981; Weikart, 1977). There are many African Americans who have conquered poverty, racism, and prejudice in the quest for success. Their resiliency can never be ignored or down-played. For instance, Weikart (1977) warned that the deficit model of thinking, when applied to a certain population (in this case, African Americans), "seems to limit potential assistance to that group because it channels thinking in ways that emphasize weaknesses rather than strengths, and it interprets differences from the norm as individual deficits" (p 175). The logical extension is that:

> We cannot limit ourselves to the identification of trait dimensions or typological classifications across individuals without also considering the characteristics of the environments within which individuals function. Nor can we limit ourselves to an analysis of the environmental determinants of human differences without also considering the hereditary determinants. Finally, we have to ask ourselves what kind of society is most desirable for the expression of human diversity—for the opportunity for each of us to grow as individuals and at the same time not infringe on the rights of others to develop their own individuality. (Minton & Schneider, 1985, p. 489)

Minton and Schneider's (1985) statements have far-reaching implications for research, policy, and practice in the general and special education of African Americans. For instance, first, research that focuses on behavior problems of African American children and youth needs to address measures that will help us to understand them. When we understand them, we assist them better to be functional, goal-directed decision makers in our complex society. Put another way, research that focuses on underlying pathological attributes of African American students needs to be valued with caution because such a research is deficit oriented and lacks measurable or observable solution-based attributes. Second, research, policy, and practice ought to go hand in glove. About three decades ago, Keogh (1990) noted that "from this perspective, policy should follow research, and change should be found in evidence" (p. 186). It is apparent that something is wrong with our intervention strategies for African American students with special needs. Third, research that divorces itself from the fundamental principles of individualized instructional programming for African American students fail to appreciate or value their unique styles and differences. This means that we need redirection in research funding and projects to reflect culturally sensitive proactive measures. Research studies with skewed divisive, emotionally loaded, political underpinnings must be discouraged in special education. Any research that does not lend itself to common-sense problem-solving interpretation and practice must be viewed with caution. Fortunately today, most scholarly publications (e.g., *Behavior Disorders*,

26 *Valuing Other Voices*

Exceptional Children, Intervention in School and Clinic, Journal of Special Education, Multicultural Learning and Teaching, Multiple Voices, Remedial and Special Education, Teacher Education and Special Education) are demanding pedagogical and practical implications to authors' works. Consequently, scholars, educators, and leaders must begin to broaden their definitions, theories, and intervention models to reduce illusory conclusions, perceptual assumptions, and prejudicial generalizations (Obiakor, 2007). African American students with special needs deserve well-prepared professionals. In fact, teacher educators and leaders must begin to realign themselves with new ways of thinking that go beyond tradition.

It has become very apparent that poorly prepared teachers teach African American learners poorly. As a result, teacher educators and leaders must practice what they preach. They must use divergent techniques to prepare future educators who will, in turn, use divergent techniques to teach African American learners who exhibit different styles, skills, and needs. To look for the "magic pill" that can cure educational problems of *all* African American students is not realistic. However, the key is for teacher educators and leaders to prepare those who value individual differences and cultural needs of these students (Ford, Obiakor, & Patton, 1995; Obiakor, 2001b, 2003, 2007; Obiakor & Beachum, 2005; Obiakor et al., 2003; Obiakor & Ford, 2002; Obiakor, Schwenn, & Rotatori, 1999; Wilder, Obiakor, & Algozzine, 2003). By so doing, they become aware of emotional first-aids needed to address crises confronting their African American students (Obiakor et al., 1997). Earlier, Price (1991) explained that it is nonproductive to bemoan new multicultural paradigms that incorporate quality and equity in educational programming. I believe we must avoid any kind of multiculturalism that tends to project "goodness" with underlying negative intentions and phony sense of community. This kind of goodness hampers ways to increase the knowledge about the interactions between human behaviors and cultural styles. To this end, teacher educators and leaders must make efforts to recruit and retain African American students, faculty, and staff to remain competitive in this age of change (Obiakor, 2001b, 2007; Obiakor & Beachum, 2005; Obiakor & Utley, 1997; Wald, 1996).

CONCLUSION

The United States has tried to institute historical policies and legal mandates to protect African American students with special needs. In addition, it has tried to provide them with equal public education. However, the interpretation and implementation of pertinent laws have garnered many loopholes that need to be sealed. The overrepresentation of CLD students (in this case, Africa Americans) in special education has continued to cause great concerns. If these students have been misplaced, it means that their educational needs cannot be met. Appropriate educational programming should be in least restrictive environments in which the race, culture, and language of African American students do not result in misidentification, misassessment, miscategorization, misplacement, and misinstruction. Based on my personal experiences, I believe the heart and soul of quality service delivery for these students must include nonrestrictive environments and settings that maximize their potential. Finally, such environments must be racially, culturally, linguistically, and socio-economically accepting.

CHAPTER 4

LEADERSHIP FOR CHANGING TIMES

In social, cultural, economic, political, and educational quarters, there appears to be some cravings for new and good leadership that values diverse voices. In many parts of the world today, traditional leaders are experiencing the wrath of the general populace because they are perceived to lack leadership for change. This is the kind of leadership that appreciates the diversity of their people. Similar problems have intensely manifested themselves from prekindergarten to university levels in the United States. For example, in education, we consistently see the victimization and silencing of "outside the box" culturally and linguistically diverse (CLD) voices. The modus vivendi has been to play games, work smart (not hard), join the herd mentality, be seen, and not be heard. In addition, we see visible leadership failures and mediocrity that are devoid of measurable checks and balances on issues related to diversity; and one is forced to ask, Who actually runs the show?

When it comes to leadership, life sometimes imitates art, and vice versa. It is frequently unreal to see the problems that CLD persons confront in education and society; and there appears to be leadership vacuums at almost all levels. Yes, there are no easy answers; yet, leadership continues to matter in our changing world. A few leadership lessons can be learned from William Shakespeare (Walter J. Black, 1944) whose phenomenal literary judgments foreshadowed many of today's critical leadership problems. For instance, in his play, *Macbeth*, Duncan was portrayed as a leader who trusted and relied on his followers for both personal and

---

Valuing Other Voices: Discourses That Matter in Education, Social Justice, and Multiculturalism, pp. 29–32

Copyright © 2020 by Information Age Publishing
All rights of reproduction in any form reserved.

30 *Valuing Other Voices*

national protection. Duncan was also a passive and weak leader who relied so much on a few trusted voices—he never wanted to take charge. Macbeth, one of his able and trusted soldiers betrayed and killed him even as he bestowed him with more honors. However, killing Duncan did not bring peace to Macbeth and his dubious wife. Like many of today's leaders, Macbeth wanted to be a king by any means necessary; however, his success in killing Duncan motivated him to kill more so that he would reign as king for a long time, confirming the predictions of the three weird sisters or witches. In the end, his wife died and he was killed miserably; and in his sorrow, he acknowledged that "life's like a walking shadow" and that "it's like a tale told by an idiot full of sound and fury, yet signifying nothing." Looking at some of today's traditional leaders and borrowing from William Shakespeare's *Macbeth*, it is important to wonder why these so-called leaders do not care about change or how posterity will remember them, especially on how they addressed the plights of disenfranchised, disadvantaged, and disillusioned CLD learners.

VISION AND LEADERSHIP: THE RELATIONSHIP

More than a decade ago, Kouzes and Posner (2007) posited that good leaders must be honest, forward-looking (visionary), inspiring, and competent. These characteristics are uniquely important for leaders in today's changing world. Leadership is not about firing or hiring people; it is about having the vision that fosters a collaborative, consultative, and cooperative environment. Obviously, this kind of environment must value diversity and embrace the comprehensive support model so as to energize students, families, educational professionals (e.g., teachers and leaders), community members, and government agencies (Obiakor, 2001, 2008). As indicated, good leaders must have a clear vision. Interestingly, many years ago, this view was noted by McFarland, Senn, and Childress (1993) in their book, *21st Century Leadership: Dialogue With 100 Top Leaders*. They argued that:

> a clear vision for an organization unifies and inspires. Employees become self-motivated to be a part of the vision and move in that direction. People laboring under the weight of cumbersome hierarchy and ponderous procedures find their efforts often frustrated and their personal initiative crushed. In contrast, it quickly becomes apparent that people have much more to offer when they are self-driven and produce within the context of a powerful vision. (p. 95)

Logically, a good leader must believe in people (Tucker, 1984). In his book, *On Becoming a Leader*, the former President of the University of

Cincinnati, Warren Bennis (1989) acknowledged that a good leader must (a) master the context, (b) understand the basics, (c) know himself/herself, (d) know the world, (e) operate on instinct, (f) deploy himself/herself—strike hard and try everything, (g) move through chaos, (h) get people on his/her side, (i) understand that this can help or hinder, and (j) forge the future. In consonance, Tim Solso, the chief executive officer of Cummins, a global power company recalled three fundamental lessons that he learned from his father: "to treat all people with dignity and respect, to do your best every time and to be true to yourself and your personal values" (Bolsta, 2008, p. 62). Clearly, vision must be about working with different people to have a unity of purpose and to achieve a common good.

EMBRACING "CHANGE" IN AN ERA OF COMPLEXITY

Educational professionals and leaders must be challenged to embrace change and an era of change. School policies and programs must respond to the changing times. For example, current systems of student identification, assessment/accountability, categorization/labeling, placement, and instruction must be consistently revisited, especially as they pertain to CLD learners. We need to hear more CLD voices in the leadership circles. As I indicated elsewhere (Obiakor, 2001, 2008), one-dimensional thinking has never yielded the desired dividends in education and related professions. We need truly good leaders who are open-minded and not those who divide and conquer. In addition, we need leaders who can prepare new leaders and not those who specialize in destroying new voices that they might find heretical. From prekindergarten to university levels, we have seen leaders who are always "inside the box." These so-called leaders masquerade their bigotry as they pride themselves on being members of a team or what I call the "sinking ship." In addition, these leaders are poisonous vision-less elements who seek to destroy new ideas that disrupt their equilibrium. And, when they are threatened, they become even more dangerous. Systems that keep these leaders are equally as dangerous as the leaders they preserve. No paradigm shifts in education when such leaders are in charge. This is the more reason why most visionary organizations do not compromise *quality and equity*.

It is critical that school leaders endeavor to build sailing ships and not sinking ships. Obiakor and Algozzine (2011a) agreed that the sinking ship drowns its occupants! "While multicultural education requires painstaking sacrifice, altruism, dedication, and commitment at all educational levels ... it can be achieved and it must be achieved" (see Obiakor& Algozzine, 2011b, p. 4). Through their actions, some leaders have been false prophets of multiculturalism. Many of them "shamelessly use

32 *Valuing Other Voices*

their ill-gotten power, privilege, and influence to (a) intimidate and patronize CLD faculty; (b) "talibanize" new thinking in general and special education; (c) perpetuate traditional misidentification, misassessment, miscategorization, misplacement, and misinstruction; (d) devalue educational quality and equity; and (e) silent and destroy dissenting voices" (see Obiakor& Algozzine, 2011b, p. 4). I believe school leaders and professionals must infuse the kind of education that creates opportunities, opens doors, expands villages, reduces tribalizations, builds bridges, eliminates racism, engenders trusts, improves collaborative consultations, and grows our future generation.

CONCLUSION

As a whole, I believe our educational programs need new kinds of leaders. These new leaders are those who can challenge themselves as they embrace change. They are also those who understand that if they do not change, they will be consumed by change. The days for passive leadership are gone. People want leaders who are visionary, value their personal idiosyncratic behaviors, listen to them, and grow with them. Such leaders must understand what is going on outside their own world and embrace the realities of others. In other words, such leaders must be good students and good followers and must be willing to respond to external stimuli and all stakeholders. Clearly, current changes in our classrooms, schools, communities, regions, states, nation, and world call for leaders who are open-minded and willing to shift their paradigms; we do not need weak leaders or over-zealous leaders are unpredictable or untrustworthy.

Finally, as a change agent, I am convinced that we need pragmatic leaders who believe in learning and doing. Simply, we need true leaders who can uplift our humanity. In our institutions, we cannot afford leaders who believe in fake news or alternative facts. And, we cannot afford mushroom leaders, fraudulent multiculturalists, myopic thinkers, and racist xenophobes who play sophomoric political games to gain and keep power. To a large extent, we need honest leaders with integrity and good moral compass. In the end, we need futuristic leaders who are dynamic consensus builders, powerful team players, and exemplary collaborators.

CHAPTER 5

BEYOND SILENCE IN SOCIAL JUSTICE AND MULTICULTURALISM

Some years ago, the Nigerian Nobel Prize Winner in Literature, Wole Soyinka (1994), a man from the Yoruba tribe of Nigeria, noted that "the man [woman] dies" in anyone "who keeps silence in the face of tyranny." This powerful statement is a part of the title of the book that he wrote when he was unfairly jailed for challenging the inhumane treatment and pogrom against the Ibos in Nigeria. Even though he was in danger of losing his life, he refused to be silenced and never gave up (see Soyinka, 1994). All over the world, his historical statement has set positive practical precedence for multiculturalists, freedom fighters, whistle blowers, and social justice advocates, to name a few.

The problems in our world today call for revisiting the word *silence* as a tool for advancing or retarding our progress as humans. Some people see *silence* as a construct that embodies wisdom, calmness, humility, low key attitude, and obedience. And, others view *silence* as cowardice, ignorance, dumb, and stoic. In reality, it is not easy to define the construct, *silence* since definitions are frequently based on personal experiences and interpretations. Despite these multidimensional interpretations, *silence* is a powerful construct that is tied to the apron string of illusory sociocultural generalizations. In this regard, one is forced to ask some pertinent questions. Without silence, will freedom, civil rights, and justice be achieved by the disenfranchised, disadvantaged, and disillusioned in any community

---

Valuing Other Voices: Discourses That Matter in Education, Social Justice, and Multiculturalism, pp. 33–37

Copyright © 2020 by Information Age Publishing

All rights of reproduction in any form reserved.

34 *Valuing Other Voices*

and society? Will the dominant powers and forces relinquish their powers or listen to the masses out of their own goodwill without noise, opposition, and resistance? Does the man/woman die or remain magnanimous when he/she keeps silent in the face of wickedness, humiliation, and destruction of hateful, powerful, and dominant peoples, tribes, races, religions, and so on? And, how can we move our humanity forward in this changing and complex world if we remain silent?

It is common knowledge that *silence* is very much valued by "bad" and "good" people. Sometimes, our equilibrium is disrupted when we encounter aggressive advocates, agitators, and noise makers. We get very irritated when they ask too many questions or raise hell while asking them. We call them names and make derogatory remarks about them. To describe them, we use statements like, "empty vessels make the most noise." In the end, we make all kinds of negative efforts to *silence* these noise makers and hell-raisers. Sadly, these are exactly what racist people, dominant tribes, dictatorial leaders, and military juntas do—they use different communication and media outlets to market their puritanical resolves and brutalize or intimidate their citizens, and expect or force them to be silent. When people are silenced, they walk around afraid and obey laws and regulations that fail to respect or value their dignity or humanity. On the other hand, some good people believe in natural law that suggests "what will be, will be." These individuals glorify *silence* and believe "we should let the sleeping dogs lie" and "it's unnecessary to flog a dead horse." Without thinking too much about these statements, they have the problem of allowing evil and victimization to reign. Silence at some level hurts and fails to move our society forward. It is no surprise that Martin Luther King Jr. (1957) eloquently noted that "we will remember not the words of our enemies, but the silence of our friends." Remarkably, he repeated this statement in various forms and put himself on the line for abuse many times (King, 1967). Though he was finally assassinated, he remains honorable today and generationally.

SPEAKING OUT TO ADVANCE SOCIAL JUSTICE AND MULTICULTURALISM

While *silence* is graceful in some situations, it can be damaging in other situations. One's *silence* can abet victimization intentionally or unintentionally. Interestingly, cowardly bullies can use *silence* to reaffirm their superiority and supremacy over others. In addition, these bullies can use *silence* to determine who is in or out in their respective organizations. For example, I have seen many White colleagues who have suffered from victimization themselves because they tried to support a culturally and

Beyond Silence in Social Justice and Multiculturalism   35

linguistically diverse (CLD) student, colleague, or leader. These colleagues are called names like "nigger lovers" because they dared to have integrity in the work place. In addition, I have been in meetings where my voice was ignored and made to feel invisible (Ellison, 1952). When I am in such meetings, I feel diminished, unwanted, and unvalued. No human being should be made to feel diminished, unwanted, and unvalued whether he/she is rich, poor, Muslim, Christian, White, Black, Latino, Asian, Native American, to mention a few. Any kind of forced *silence* has far-reaching devastating consequences.

It is critical that we know what happens to CLD people in White dominant organizations. Simply, people are required to "toe the line" since organizations have implicit and explicit rules and regulations. Anyone who steps outside the box faces the wrath of colleagues and supervisors. In other words, people, especially those who are different are forced to be silent. When voices are forced to be silent, social justice advocates suffer. For example, it is not uncommon to hear CLD individuals indicate publicly that they have not experienced racism and victimization in their respective organizations to please their White colleagues and supervisors. They find themselves in precarious positions and expose their "warring souls," hoping that their colleagues and supervisors will value them and find them less threatening. As a result, while quality performance is always highlighted, the silent ones are viewed as those who fit in and promoted because they fit in. The results are that (a) creativities are stifled, (b) quality becomes a lip service, (c) the environment becomes a toxic "dog-eat-dog" environment, (d) CLD attributes are minimized and disrespected, (e) phony communities are built, (f) fraudulent multiculturalism flourishes, and (g) all kinds of unsafe organizational gaps are created.

Clearly, we must embrace change as a part of our lives. Speaking out to advance social justice and multiculturalism is extremely important. Since change does not just happen, we must speak out to foster it. But, we must be prudent in speaking out. In other words, to win the race, we must stay in the race. We must be involved to make a difference in the lives of others. In addition, we cannot afford to be victims all the time; and by the same token, we cannot afford to pretend that racism or discrimination is over. In the end, we must be proactive in combating hatred of all types in whatever we do and in whatever institutions we are connected with.

MOVING FORWARD

It is critical that we move forward with the understanding that speaking out is not just something to do; it is the right thing to do. We must be futuristic in our thinking and our actions. Consider the following

36 *Valuing Other Voices*

examples. Despite the risks involved and the victimizations that I have endured as a scholar, educator, leader, and professional, I have continued to use my voice to advance multiculturalism and social justice at all educational levels. Wole Soyinka spoke out by using his national/global prominence and literary talents to voice his opposition of pogrom against the Ibos during the Nigeria/Biafra war. Martin Luther King Jr. spoke out against the racist victimization of African Americans and other disadvantaged people in the United States. Malcolm X put his life on the line to advocate intensely about the subjugation of African Americans in the American society. Marcus Garvey risked being thrown out of America to speak out about the freedoms of Black people all over the world. Rosa Park spoke out for civil rights of African Americans by refusing to sit behind the bus. Thurgood Marshall used his legal prowess to reduce discrimination and foster civil rights in the United States. And, Nelson Mandela, Desmond Tutu, and the host of others from South Africa took the risk to speak out for the elimination of apartheid in South Africa. In fact, many others have used different dimensions of uplifting actions to fight for the freedoms of vulnerable peoples all over the world.

To move forward, it is important that we understand that people of all races and creeds have used (and continue to use) their talents, positions, opportunities, and actions to speak out against the victimization of atypical peoples. We must also understand the intricacies of race, skin color, culture, language, national origin, religion, socioeconomics, and gender, to mention a few. In addition, we must not deny the existence of discrimination or bigotry because we have not experienced its devastating effects ourselves. In the end, we must understand that multiculturalism and social justice will not advance in any organization or in any part of the world without good-hearted advocacies by determined risk takers who have refused to be silent.

As we move forward, we must ask the hard questions and engage in fearless conversations on critical socioeducational issues in our professions. In addition, we must continue to search for unending *truths* on issues such as the (a) misidentification, misassessment, miscategorization, misplacement, and misinstruction of CLD students; (b) high suspension and expulsion rates of CLD students; (c) police brutality, police shooting/killing, and unfair imprisonment of African Americans; (d) misperception of immigrants in our society; (e) invisibility of CLD teachers in our pre-K–12 schools; and (f) lack of proactive recruitment, retention, tenure, and promotion of CLD faculty, staff, and leaders in our colleges and universities. Indeed, the *silence* of CLD and vulnerable people in all sectors of our society is disgraceful, demeaning, and devaluing. We must turn this situation around by allowing more voices to be heard in our respective organizations and institutions. We need creative programs that encourage unity, valuing, and respect at all levels—our goal must be to encourage "hearty" conversations that reduce tribalization, victimization, and racialization (Obiakor, 2018). The time is now because our society's future is at stake! If we do not speak out today, who will speak out for us?

CONCLUSION

While *silence* can be interpreted from multiple perspectives, it can help or hurt an individual or organization. Also, it can be misconstrued. It is important to remember that the world failed to speak out early when Hitler was engaging in the pogrom of the Jewish people in Germany. And, through the years, many Hitlerlike leaders have used their powers to victimize their citizens and the world. Today, we see leaders who are brutal and rude to their fellow citizens; and yet, we fail to react with alacrity to their inhumanity. The good news is that some determined citizens are not giving up in risking their lives and careers to react to hateful domineering behaviors. This means that we must continue to be vigilant, speak out, and let our voices heard to respond to the racist, xenophobic, and antimulticultural elements of our society. To be successful in our efforts, we must collaborate, consult, and cooperate as needed. Our society loses when divisive Individuals win!

Finally, it is time that we began to challenge ourselves again in order to make our world a better and safe place to live. We appear skeptical about our future and seem overwhelmed by conflicts, wars, terrorism, racism, xenophobia, and hatred, to mention a few. It is counterproductive to just sit down, cross our hands, and do nothing—we must speak out and do what we can to reduce the impacts of the aforementioned problems on our fellow humans. In addition, we must stop blaming others for these problems; we are all to blame when we nonchalantly condone injustice. Our overall goal must be to solve endemic societal problems that confront and divide us. We can no longer afford to remain silent and allow our world to be destroyed by the selfish ends of a few of us. In the end, we must take the bull by its horns by speaking out boldly and wisely and by resisting the temptation to be silent in the face of injustice! In the words of Soyinka (1994), "The man [woman] dies in him [her] who keeps silence in the face of tyranny."

CHAPTER 6

THE "MODEL MINORITY MYTH" AND ASIANS IN AMERICA'S HIGHER EDUCATION

Impact on Multicultural Education

As a minority in the United States, I am always troubled when people view me as a "good Black." While it is unclear what a good Black means, I know that it is prone to confusions and misinterpretations. To have an in-depth picture of what the phrase meant, I asked my late fraternity brother, hero, mentor, and well-known scholar and educator, Dr. Asa Hilliard Jr. (Personal communication, April 12, 1991) during one of our meetings at an international convention. He told me that that was one of oldest racist tricks in the world—it occurs when a member of the dominant society, in this case, a White person classifies a minority positively and patronizingly as better than people of his/her race to appear friendly and accepting. As Dr. Hilliard Jr. (1991) indicated, the underlying thinking is that I can now escape the negative perceptions of other African peoples, in this case, African Americans because I have now been accepted by the "master" or the dominant power. He further noted that historically African Americans are negatively perceived to be "lazy, poor, unintelligent, retarded, violent, criminally minded, immoral, repugnant, troublesome, unfriendly, drug addicted, untrustworthy, unpatriotic, unreliable, and unmotivated," to

Valuing Other Voices: Discourses That Matter in Education, Social Justice, and Multiculturalism, pp. 39–46
Copyright © 2020 by Information Age Publishing
All rights of reproduction in any form reserved.

40 *Valuing Other Voices*

mention a few. Dr. Hilliard Jr. (1991) concluded that some Blacks actually appreciate being known as good Blacks. I found this to be a sad commentary that someone will value derogatory remarks about his race and people just to be valued and accepted by others. This also gave me an insight into why Asians in America are viewed as model minorities and why some of them accept that label. As a result, I felt inspired to revisit how my interactions with Asians in America's higher education have revealed the "model minority myth" and how this myth has contextually impacted multicultural understanding and valuing.

I very much respect the work habits and cultural values of Asians based on my interactions with them all over the world. I have been taught by them; I have gone to school with them; I have worked with them; and I have taught and mentored them. They have been amazing in their contributions to any society that they have been involved with. My goal here is not to judge Asians or belittle their capabilities, my intension is to analyze the model minority myth and how this myth has influenced the advancement of multicultural education in America's higher education. Yes, I am a non-Asian who does not pretend to know all Asians. And, my consistent thinking is that like other culturally and linguistically diverse (CLD) persons, Asians are peoples of different intelligences, cultures, values, and perspectives (Sue & Sue, 2008) that deserve exposition, valuation, and appreciation.

I came in contact with Asians in Nigeria, my country of origin. As an undergraduate student in college, I had many professors from India. I found them to be very intelligent and caring; they had tremendous impact on me. In fact, two of them became my powerful references when I began the application process to continue my graduate education in the United States. After my undergraduate education, I became a high school teacher to earn some money to get me prepared for my education in the United States. During this period, I played tennis with a Filipino medical doctor who regularly came to exercise with me. We became friends; however, I found his friendship to be interesting—he never wanted to associate in depth with me even when I tried. Since my father was a businessman who imported plates/enamels from Hong Kong, I got to know how the people of Hong Kong behaved, interacted, and did business. Also, in the city where we lived, we got to know some Chinese people who worked in the textile factories as supervisors. Again, these Chinese people were friendly, but never engaged in deep friendship with the people around them. I was very bothered by this kind of behavior and asked my father about that. He advised me to ignore their behaviors and treat every human being with respect and dignity. To a large measure, my father's advice of treating all people with respect and dignity has guided my interactions with different people.

EXPERIENCES AS A GRADUATE STUDENT

When I came to the United States, I began my graduate program at Texas Christian University, Fort Worth, Texas. Interestingly, my roommate was from India—he was pursuing his graduate degree in business administration. We were both serious students who performed superbly in school; and we both knew that. So, we had mutual respect for each other. We were all very active members of the International Students Association at Texas Christian University. The president of the association was also from India; I found him to be an interesting character. He consistently told me that he was a Caucasian—I was shocked that he had such a strange mentality. He acted superior when he interacted with students from Africa and other developing countries—he was arrogant and felt superior all the time. As a result, most of us began to view him as a "White tool." It became clear to me that he was engaging in the model minority myth, a model that views Asians to be more academically and intellectually superior than Whites or other CLD people (Chow, 2017; Feagin &Chou, 2008; Li & Wang, 2008).

When I went to New Mexico State University, Las Cruces, New Mexico to continue my PhD degree, I was glad to have an Asian American female professor in my department. She was married to a White male professor in another department in the College of Education. She seemed to command immense respect from her colleagues and students and later was made the department head. Her initial interactions with me were great— I respected her as a nationally known scholar and as someone who was politically astute. It is no wonder that I chose her to be a member of my doctoral committee; and she was excellent and supportive in her role. While I doubt that she intentionally viewed herself as a model minority, I am convinced that some of her colleagues and students viewed her as a model minority. I observed how they spoke about her—she was patronized a lot! Before long, she went to another university to serve as associate dean and my interactions with her never quite bloomed. Sadly, as qualified and amazing as she was, I doubt if she ever got to be a dean. In the end, she had a powerful impact on my life, just from observing her as a professor and department head and reading her works as a scholar.

Looking back at my experiences in Nigeria, at Texas Christian University, and at New Mexico State University, I can say that I had some good and "not-so-good" experiences in my dealings with Asians. In my interactions, I found that Asians cannot be judged as a group—it is wrong to view all Asians as the same. It is crystal clear that Asians, like others, are different in behavior, personal idiosyncrasy, religion, academic achievement, intellectual capacity, and socioeconomic status, to mention a few. It is dangerously unproductive and condescending to identify, assess, and catego-

42 *Valuing Other Voices*

rize them prejudicially and make illusory generalizations about them (Sue & Sue, 2008).

EXPERIENCES AS A PROFESSOR

When I landed an assistant professor position at Rust College, Holly Springs, Mississippi, I was impressed with the number of Asian professors at the college. They were dedicated professors who came originally from India, Middle East, East Asia, and a host of other Asiatic nations. They cared for their students and seemed to feel at home in this historically Black college environment. Interestingly, they were viewed as model minorities. For some strange reason, I thought that they were treated with more respect than their foreign-born African colleagues. When I moved to the University of Tennessee, Chattanooga (UTC), I had no Asian or Asian American colleagues or students in my department; and I was very bothered by this. For three years that I was there, I advocated for the recruitment of Asian faculty and for broadening our student recruitment processes; and my advocacy was met with intense resistance. I left the University of Tennessee for Henderson State University at Arkadelphia, Arkansas where I saw a similar sad picture. I left Henderson for Emporia State University, Emporia, Kansas where I saw some frantic efforts by some faculty members and some members of the administrative team to recruit Asian students and faculty, despite the university's first female president's closemindedness and racist tendencies. This was welcomed news in my eyes; however, the efforts did not materialize to having an Asian colleague in my department.

After about 6 years at Emporia State University, I went to the University of Wisconsin-Milwaukee as a senior scholar. During this period, I met Dr. Philip Chinn, an Asian and a well-known and respectable scholar in general and special education, at an international conference. He told me the unforgettable racist treatment that he received when he interviewed for a job at the University of Wisconsin-Milwaukee—he noted that he was still bitter and advised me to be very careful about racism in that university. He was right because the racism that I experienced and endured there was blatant! In my department, we finally recruited an Asian female professor. And, as-coordinator of graduate program, I recruited one student from India and another from China. Many of my colleagues did not appreciate that—they doubted the quality and capability of these students. Before long, they began to take the credit for recruiting the same students and also began to use the Asian female professor and other CLD faculty and students who I helped to recruit to fight against me. It was a strange and twisted triangulation—almost like the old retrogressive

The "Model Minority Myth" and Asians in America's Higher Education   43

"divide and conquer" philosophy! Sadly, some of them struggled with it, but fell for it in the end! When the Asian female professor went to another university, the department now got excited to hire (and actually hired) another Asian female professor who openly and consistently opposed me when I raised issues pertaining to multicultural recruitment, retention, and inclusion at all levels. Unfortunately, this professor totally bought into the model minority myth. During this period, I was truly reminded of the late Dr. Martin King Jr.'s (1957) eloquent statement: "we will remember not the words of our enemies, but the silence of our friends." Overall, at the University of Wisconsin-Milwaukee, I mentored many faculty members (including Asians) to successfully get tenure and promotion and many graduate students to successfully graduate from their respective programs. For example, I served as a major advisor to the first Hmong PhD student in the Department of Educational Leadership; and he impressively graduated. I felt honored that many CLD faculty members and PhD students came to me and took advantage of my strong presence as a teacher-scholar to do exemplary works. Some of them have moved on to do bigger and better things. Remarkably, I lit the candles in these individuals instead of cursing the darkness in them.

EXPERIENCES AS A DEPARTMENT HEAD/CHAIR

I accepted a job as department head at The City College of New York, City University of New York system where I saw many Asian faculty and students. Initially, I was impressed! In my research before accepting the job, I heard that an Asian American female faculty member of Chinese origin was suing the college because of tenure denial. That was a red flag to me; but, I still accepted the position because I was hoping to turn things around! When her case was settled, she became the only Asian faculty member in my department. In my conversations with her, I found her to be a smart and supportive advocate for social justice who seemed not to buy into the "model minority myth." I respected and valued her a lot because she brought so much to the table (Ogbu, 1978). In other departments of the School of Education and the college as a whole, I met and talked with a few Asian professors of Indian origin. It was difficult to develop real relationships with them. For example, one of them was very patronizing and arrogant in his statements to me—in fact, he made it clear to me that his wife was a powerful Jewish White woman; and considering the exemplary achievement and performance levels of Nigerian immigrants in the United States, I felt sick to my stomach. It became clear to me that many of these professors had assimilated the belief that they were truly model minorities (Li & Wang, 2008). Interestingly, my

44   *Valuing Other Voices*

experiences with some of these professors reminded me of the shameless arrogance and antimulticultural perspectives of Dinesh D'Souza (1996, 1998), an Indian-born conservative commentator who without proper qualifications was hired as the president of a college (i.e., The King's College, New York City) from 2010 to 2012.

When I left the City College of New York for Valdosta State University, Valdosta, Georgia to assume a position as department chair, I felt excited that I was coming back to the South where I went to school and worked for a while. We had an Asian female professor who contributed so much to the multicultural discourse in the department. As a leader and colleague, I saw that she was treated as an invisible woman. Though she was patronized a lot, she did not buy into the game; she focused her attention on doing her job superbly. In fact, some of our colleagues tried to use her to fight against me; however, she never fell for it. Before leaving Valdosta, I was fortunate to teach courses in the interdisciplinary studies division directed by the assistant provost, an Asian American woman who I found to be caring, smart, dedicated, and humane. By all measurable standards, she was remarkable and fantastic in what she did. I learned a lot from her!

In my search for deanship positions in colleges/schools of Education, I rarely saw Asians and other CLD administrators, faculty, staff, and students. It became apparent to me that there were no frantic efforts to recruit, retain, and graduate, and/or promote them. Even in places that had Asian or other CLD administrators, there appeared to be lip service. I still remember interviewing for the Prairie View A&M University, Dean of the College of Education position. The retiring dean of more than 2 decades was an Asian American of Indian origin. In my interview with him, he laughed and noted that "Nigerians are everywhere; and they can be trouble makers." I did not find this statement to be funny, especially when I think about the large populations of Indians and Asians in Nigeria and all over Africa. Clearly, he was not excited about supporting me as dean. Though I learned that the search committee gave my name to the university leadership, I was not offered the job because the former dean was not very excited about me. I was very bothered by this since this was supposed to be a predominantly Black institution.

IMPLICATIONS FOR MULTICULTURAL EDUCATION IN HIGHER EDUCATION

As someone who has been involved with America's higher education for about 4 decades, I understand the dangers and risks involved in speaking out about racism and the lack of CLD leaders, faculty, staff, and students in higher education. But, *silence* is not and will never be the answer! Some

The "Model Minority Myth" and Asians in America's Higher Education   45

years ago, the Nigerian Nobel Prize Winner in Literature, Wole Soyinka (1994), affirmed that "the man [woman] dies" in anyone "who keeps silence in the face of tyranny." All over the world, his historical statement has set positive practical precedence for multiculturalists, social justice advocates, civil rights leaders, freedom fighters, and whistle blowers, to mention a few. Some people see *silence* as a construct that embodies wisdom, calmness, humility, low key attitude, and obedience. And, others view *silence* as cowardice, ignorance, dumb, and stoic (Obiakor, 2018). In reality, it is not easy to define the construct, *silence* since definitions are frequently based on personal experiences and interpretations. In this regard, one is forced to ask some pertinent questions. With silence, will freedom, civil rights, and justice be achieved by the disenfranchised, disadvantaged, and disillusioned in any community and society? Will the dominant powers and forces relinquish their powers or listen to the masses out of their own goodwill without noise, opposition, and resistance? Does the man/woman die or remain magnanimous when he/she keeps silent in the face of wickedness, humiliation, and destruction of hateful, powerful, and dominant peoples, tribes, races, religions, and so on? And, how can we move our humanity forward in this changing and complex world if we remain silent?

I do agree that *silence* is graceful in some situations, however, it can be damaging in other situations. One's *silence* can abet victimization intentionally or unintentionally. Interestingly, cowardly bullies can use *silence* to reaffirm their superiority and supremacy over others. In addition, these bullies can use *silence* to determine who is in or out in their respective organizations (Obiakor, 2018). For example, I have seen many White colleagues who have suffered from victimization themselves because they tried to speak out in support of a CLD student, colleague, or leader. In addition, I have been in meetings where my voice was even ignored and made to feel invisible (Ellison, 1952). No human being should be made to feel diminished, unwanted, and unvalued whether he/she is rich, poor, Muslim, Christian, White, Black, Latino, Asian, and Native American, to mention a few. Any kind of forced *silence* has far-reaching devastating consequences (Obiakor, 2018).

It is critical that Asians and other CLD individuals embrace change as a part of their lives. Speaking out to advance civil rights, social justice and multiculturalism is extremely important. Since change does not just happen, they must speak out to foster it; but, they must be prudent in speaking out. In other words, to win the race, they must stay in the race. They must be involved to make a difference in the lives of others. In addition, they cannot afford to be victims all the time; and by the same token, they cannot afford to pretend that racism or discrimination is over. In the end, Asians and other CLD individuals must be proactive in combating hatred

46   *Valuing Other Voices*

of all types in whatever they do and in whatever institutions they are connected with.

CONCLUSION

The freedoms that we enjoy today are results of the efforts of others who put their careers and lives on the line. Who will advocate for our own freedoms if we do not? How will posterity remember us if we do not play our roles creditably? We need all voices, including Asian voices to secure our freedoms. We do not need the acknowledgment of the "master" for us to know that we are worthy. I believe collaboration, consultation, and cooperation between races and peoples are possible. Such interactions must be the modus vivendi and the modus operandi of all stakeholders, including Asians and other CLD persons. This means that we need Asian voices to advance multiculturalism in America's higher education. In many colleges/schools of education, their voices seem to be soft, invisible, and unheard. While some have attributed such dispositions to be culturally related (Sue & Sue, 2008), Asian voices deserve to be heard, valued, and respected! The prevalent definition of them as model minorities is a façade that needs to be debunked. They endure similar problems as other CLD students, staff, faculty, and leaders in higher education. Finally, it is time that they began to challenge themselves again in order to make the world of higher education a better and safe place that can assist them in maximizing their fullest potential and in maximizing the potential of those who come in contact with them.

CHAPTER 7

HISTORICALLY BLACK COLLEGES AND UNIVERSITIES MATTER

Impact on Teacher Preparation

For some, the greatest nemesis in the United States or even the world is to see any "goodness" come from "Blackness." All things "bad" seem to mentally come from Blackness and all things "good" seem to come from "Whiteness;" at least, xenophobic and racist individuals will have us believe that (Obiakor, 2001b). Interestingly, in some screwed up fashion, some Blacks seem to internalize these presumed imperfections, hand over their own powers to Whites as they themselves doubt their own strengths, and awkwardly believe Blacks are destined to experience disruption, disaster, and death without White paternalistic support—some Blacks play out this phenomenon in their imaginary minds and superpassive behaviors. For example, during recent elections in the United States that brought Donald Trump to the presidency, some Blacks refused to vote and helplessly believed their votes never counted. If that is the case, the recent 2017 election of Doug Jones as a Democratic Senator from Alabama after 25 years would not have been successful. Even with all the remarkable successes in the United States, some Blacks still refuse to (a) acknowledge their powers, (b) have their positive voices heard, (b) disrupt

---

Valuing Other Voices: Discourses That Matter in Education, Social Justice, and Multiculturalism, pp. 47–53
Copyright © 2020 by Information Age Publishing
All rights of reproduction in any form reserved.

48 *Valuing Other Voices*

any retrogressive status quo or equilibrium around them; and (c) engage in absolute self-determination when they experience intentional or unintentional violation of their civil rights (Obiakor, 2018).

The reality is that lots of good have come and will continue to come from Black people and their institutions. In other words, Black people have contributed so much to the United States and the world; and they will continue to do so as long as life exists. The Black skin color does not mean evil or poverty, or anything related to it. The whole theory of biological determinism has been theoretically and practically debunked time and time again (Gardner, 1993; Gould, 1981); and the days of globalizing intelligence, self-concept, determination, zest to succeed, or any natural attribute are long gone (Obiakor, 2001a, 2018). Most barriers are now being broken; and for those unbroken, frantic efforts are already underway to break them. Consider the election of Barack Obama, the first Black President of the United States, the greatest country in the world by all measurable standards. Recently, Prince Harry of the English Royal Family became engaged to be married to Meghan Markle, a Black woman; and for the first time, the engaged couple enjoyed Christmas celebrations with the Queen of England. And, there is more to come! Naturally, we may not all be on equal footing; but given equitable opportunities, all barriers will somehow be broken as long as life exists. It is a matter of time! For those who believe in putting Black people in their place, their dreams and aspirations might seem plausible in the short run, but not materialize in the long run. So, the existence of and the productive endeavors of Blacks or HBCUs in the United States is unproductive, wrong, ignorant, malicious, diabolic, and a hollow fantasy!

HBCUS: SUCCESSES DESPITE THE ODDS

There are historically Black colleges and universities (HBCUs) in many parts of the United States; and they continue to be national and international treasures that achieve their strategic goals, vision, mission, and core values. For a long time, these institutions have perennially endured (a) discriminatory funding by the government, legislators, and agencies, (b) disruptive low expectations, (c) poor leadership and administrations, (d) self-destructive political thinking, and (e) negative press and perceptions. Yet, they have continued to grow despite the odds against them—they have continued to produce great college leaders, military leaders, educators, scholars, district superintendents, city mayors, medical doctors, nurses, pharmacists, dentists, intellectuals, engineers, astronauts, scientists, professors, researchers, politicians, lawyers, athletes, entertainers, movie producers, writers, actors, poets, to mention a few. Consider just

Historically Black Colleges and Universities Matter   49

three powerful examples from Lincoln University of Pennsylvania, an HBCU in the United States. Thurgood Marshall was the first African American justice who served as associate justice of the Supreme Court of the United States from 1967–1991; Kwame Nkrumah was the first prime minister and president of Ghana, West Africa—he worked hard for Ghana's independence; and Nnamdi Azikiwe was the first president of Nigeria, West Africa—he worked hard for Nigeria's independence. Clearly, voices of HBCUs have been heard far and wide; and these voices can never be silenced or be made invisible (Ellison, 1972).

HBCUs have been traditionally known for culturally responsive student mentoring techniques. Since many of the students who attend these institutions are first generation college students who may come from disadvantaged, disenfranchised, and disillusioned environments, they need different techniques. The ACT and SAT scores of these students do not reflect their intelligence and capability—their scores may not be as high as those of students admitted into predominantly White colleges/universities. HBCUs have consistently differentiated instruction for their students; and more often than not, they manipulate their students' learning environments to maximize their educational potential. In these institutions, they see their students' colors, but use the colors that they see as strengths. Though these institutions are not perfect, they go beyond what White institutions do—they see multiple intelligences and use them to develop their students. Consider the case of Student X below:

The Case of Student X

Student X attended a high school in a rural southern state. His parents were not very educated, but they were supportive. When his father ran into troubles with the law, the mother tried her best to raise him and his siblings. As Student X noted, "we were told to take an examination; we did not know what it was all about; and we still took it. There was no practice and my scores were too poor that I am even ashamed to give them to you." Student X was admitted to an HBCU—he knew that he was poorly prepared for college. But, because of the serious mentoring program at this HBCU, he graduated and was admitted to a master's degree program. He finished the master's program and gained admission to a well-known Research I university in the Midwest. Though he struggled in writing, he came in contact with his fraternity brother who agreed to mentor him. While serving as a lieutenant in the National Guard, he graduated with a PhD degree and has since published more than 20 publications, including refereed articles and books. He is now a very successful superintendent of a reputable school district in the Midwest. Student X's brother had similar high school and test score experiences. His brother has since earned his master's degree and has had a distinguished career in the United States military. In 2010, as a colonel, he received the Meritorious Service Award at the NAACP's National

50   *Valuing Other Voices*

Convention. Student X's brother currently works in the Pentagon. Today, both Student X and his brother have received honors for making a difference in their respective communities. They continue to mentor at-risk youth; and in their spare time, they recruit students for their alma mater.

RESPONDING TO CHANGING TIMES

An analysis of the case of Student X above makes it clear that Student X and his brother are successful patriotic leaders in today's changing world. Imagine the world that fails to give them opportunities because they are Blacks or because they scored very low on their ACT or SAT standardized test! That would have been a world not ready for the changing times! Dewey (1958) correctly noted that for education to be education, it has to be a continuous process of growth. This means that change is an important and indispensable part of education from prekindergarten to college/university levels, including HBCUs. This notion was corroborated by Friedman and Mandelbaum (2012) in their bestselling book, *That Used to Be Us: How America Fell Behind in the World It Invented and How We Can Come Back* when they wrote:

> America needs to close two education gaps at once. We need to close the gap between black, Hispanic, and other minority students and the average for white students on standardized reading, writing, and math tests. But we have an equally dangerous gap between the average American student and the average students in many industrial countries that we consider collaborators, and competitors, including Singapore, Korea, Taiwan, Finland, and those in the most developed parts of China. (p.111)

Looking at the 21st century, some logical conclusions emerge from the aforementioned details. First, if we do not change, we will be consumed by change. Second, standardized tests are not good predictor variables of how successful a student can be in school or in life. Third, the environment that students learn in is critical to their success or failure. Fourth, poverty does not mean "poor" self-determination or poor zest to succeed in school or in life. And fifth, culturally responsible techniques work for many students who are at-risk. But, there are other loaded conclusions that one can deduct from the above details. If the United States intends to continue its status as a world power, it must stop (a) looking down on its citizens because of their skin color, national origin, race, gender, socioeconomic status, ability, disability, culture, language, religion, or personal idiosyncrasy; (b) playing the politics of race when it comes to funding HBCUs; and (c) downplaying the talented students, professors, scholars, and leaders who operate within the confines of HBCUs.

On the other hand, if HBCUs intend to maintain and strengthen their reputation, their "powers that be" must be (a) self-analytical in selecting visionary board of trustee members who are above board; (b) prudent in hiring creative presidents and servant leaders who are psychologically strong to recruit, retain, and promote outstanding people; (c) recruit proactive people who value good teaching, good scholarship, and good professional service; (d) astute in divorcing themselves from myopic political mentality that says, "I got mine, you go get yours;" and (e) proud of their historical achievements and market themselves properly to respond to the changing times.

IMPACT ON TEACHER PREPARATION IN HBCUS

It is no more debatable that HBCUs are proud historical institutions of the United States. I believe they should treat themselves that way so that others will treat them the way that they want to be treated. They cannot afford to flounder in mediocrity or allow others to determine their future. They need to be competitive in recruiting powerful professors, scholars, and professionals, especially in their teacher preparation programs. In most cases, they prepare teachers and professionals who are consistently needed in urban and inner-city areas. HBCUs cannot afford to dumb down their College/School of Education programs and expect to be respected at the same time.

The moral imperative must be to help anyone who sets foot on any teacher preparation program at an HBCU to maximize his/her fullest potential, whether he/she is a student, faculty, or leader. In the end, this means that productivity must be honored, respected, rewarded, and treated as a modus vivendi by all stakeholders. Simply put, the crab-bucket syndrome must be discouraged, especially since it dumbs down quality and punishes productive members of the department or college/school.

Teacher preparation programs at HBCUs must keep their powders dry. These programs must make frantic efforts to:

- reconcile their vision and mission to societal demands—what they do must be current and cutting and be reflected in their websites;
- respond to demographic shifts in power and paradigms—they must be multicultural and global in nature as they respond to student, staff, faculty, leadership, and programmatic issues;
- encourage professional development and improvement—they must reward those who attend conferences to know cutting-edge issues,

52 *Valuing Other Voices*

present papers, and engage in scholarly activities (e.g., publishing refereed articles and books) to market themselves;

- search for resources and funds to create new programs and invest in programs that are growing—they must reward grant writers and project directors to motivate them to do more;

- work with internal and external stakeholders—they must work with teacher mentors and cooperating teachers and involve community members in advisory boards or committees to hear their voices.

- encourage partnerships and interdisciplinary efforts—they must practice what they preach to build collaboration, consultation, and cooperation and grow inter-departmental relations and projects;

- stop playing the same games that they accuse predominantly White institutions of playing—they must demonstrate that they are against the silencing and invisibility of other voices that force people to lose faith in the system. For students, they must use culturally responsive strategies that will inspire them to be the best that they can be; and

- build conscientious communities where people can call home— they must believe in "quality with a heart" where people engage in fearless or "hearty" conversations and still get their tenure and promotion. In the end, this will truly help HBCUs to (a) retain quality students, faculty, staff, and leaders; and (b) avoid being used as training grounds for other colleges/universities.

CONCLUSION

Black people and their institutions will continue to be relevant in our society and world. Efforts to downplay them are self-destructive and not futuristic. To survive and excel in the 21st century, it is critical that HBCUs are respected, valued, and honored. In addition, we must respect, value, and honor teacher preparation programs in these colleges and universities. It is important that these programs take advantage of the talents that are on their campuses. For me, teaching at one of those programs in the early beginnings of my career was one of the greatest opportunities that I have had in my life. I learned a lot about my "Blackness" and the "Blackness" of other Black people. I was so impressed that I became a member of Omega Psi Phi Fraternity, one of the best decisions that I have made in my life. Since then, I have interviewed to be a dean in a couple of HBCUs—my experiences during these interviews have been particularly interesting, to say the least. My conclusion is that if these programs intend to remain relevant and continue to produce new, qualified, and well-prepared teachers, they must be bold in recruiting, retaining, and promoting quality high-powered professors and leaders, even if they come from predominantly White institutions. Clearly, they must be willing to compete because that is the world in which we live today.

CHAPTER 8

GLOBAL LEARNING AND TEACHING IN GENERAL AND SPECIAL EDUCATION

More than 3 decades ago, Collins and Zakariya (1982) rightly wrote:

> We live, like it or not, in an era of global interdependence. Nations rely on one another for new materials, food stuffs, consumer items, energy sources, technology, and the know-how to produce and use all of these—the tangible goods and services, in other words, that add up to international commerce. But we are equally, though perhaps less tangibly, dependent on one another for knowledge, for power, for protection, and for appreciation of the diversity of peoples and customs that are all part of our world. (p. 2)

The aforementioned statement of decades ago remains apparently relevant today. We are witnessing a tremendous worldwide expansion, which to a large measure makes our world smaller and smaller in its interactions. Even more, the larger world is made smaller by technological advancements. For example, a soccer match on November 14, 2017 between Argentina and Nigeria that saw Nigeria comeback from a dramatic two goals deficit to win the game 4–2 was happily seen at the same time by family members in Nigeria and the United States. Additionally, it is not uncommon for family members in Nigeria and Jamaica to be aware of the happenings in the United States and the world over because of Internet sources and avenues. The great international spirits that led to the creation of the United Nations Scientific and Cultural Organization

Valuing Other Voices: Discourses That Matter in Education, Social Justice, and Multiculturalism, pp. 55–59
Copyright © 2020 by Information Age Publishing
All rights of reproduction in any form reserved.

56 *Valuing Other Voices*

and the United Nations Children's Educational Fund are still alive and well. As a result, concerns about global illiteracy, hunger, poverty, diseases, wars, terrorism, xenophobia, and lack of opportunities for disenfranchised and vulnerable persons continue to resonate among peoples of the world. Even with today's human crises and stressors, many people are still willing to light the candles for the progress of the global village instead of cursing its darkness.

In recent years, many general and special educational organizations have been reaching out to their culturally and linguistically diverse (CLD) or international memberships by initiating professional divisions that appeal to issues affecting them. For example, in 1990, the Council for Exceptional Children created the Division of Culturally and Linguistically Diverse Exceptional Learners and the Division of International Special Education and Services to spread its wings nationally and globally with regard issues pertinent to special education. Many of these educational organizations now have international chapters (e.g., the International Reading Association). At the Council for Exceptional Children international conventions, it is no more unusual to see participants and memberships from Nigeria, South Africa, Bermuda, Jamaica, Canada, Mexico, China, South Korea, Turkey, Israel, Egypt, Kuwait, England, Spain, Romania, Russia, England, Spain, Germany, Austria, to mention a few. Professional and human relationships, friendships, and interactions are built and developed beyond conference locations. Ironically, while there continues to be international visibilities of foreign entities at conference levels, there also continues to be some apparent lack of knowledge in the United States about happenings in other parts of the world. As an example, the U.S. president, Donald Trump in a recent 2018 White House immigration discussion on Deferred Action for Childhood Arrivals asked, "Why are we having all these people from shithole countries come here?" Trump wondered why people from Norway are not given immigration opportunities as he denigrated Haiti and African countries, with special focus on Nigeria. Trump's xenophobic "shithole" statement was vehemently decried at worldwide levels. For example, the African Union responded by noting, "The African Union mission wishes to express its infuriation, disappointment and outrage over the unfortunate comment made by Mr. Donald Trump, the President of the United States, whose remarks dishonor the celebrated American creed and respect for diversity and human dignity." Sadly, Mr. Trump and his xenophobic supporters seem to have forgotten that pride comes with prejudice; and prejudice comes with illusory generalizations and unwarranted emotional assumptions that lead to unhealthy tribalization, nativist actions, and other forms of discriminatory divisions and practices.

Global Learning and Teaching in General and Special Education   57

The internationalization of organizations such as the Council for Exceptional Children is an excellent idea; however, they cannot be international organizations if international voices are invisible in progressive activities of these organizations. As a teacher educator, scholar, and professional leader, I have often wondered why there is a dearth of positive television news about Africa in the United States. Funny enough, Africans are frequently shown on television as helpless, hungry, and vulnerable people who are always saved by White people, missionaries, or professionals. Is it any surprise that African teachers, professors, and leaders in public schools, colleges/universities, and organizations in the United States consistently receive poor or negative evaluations and comments in their jobs? Consider the case of a school principal who visited Guatemala in Latin America for a brief vacation. Upon returning, she was asked if she enjoyed her trip and she responded: "I enjoyed my trip. But, I was frustrated because they did not speak English. If Guatemalans need our American money, they better speak English." This naïve statement is problematic and leads to more educational questions with significant multicultural implications. First, how can this principal work with immigrant students who are culturally and linguistically different? Second, how can she work with parents who come from different CLD backgrounds? Third, how can she recruit, retain, and work with teachers and related professionals who come from CLD backgrounds? And fourth, how can she work with CLD community members and stakeholders? These are critical questions that must be answered by general and special educators, school leaders, and community members if we are going to honestly build conscientious communities that value all voices, including those voices that are traditionally disenfranchised, disadvantaged, and disillusioned (Obiakor, 2018). Based on the aforementioned case, professional developments are absolutely necessary in educational and professional preparation programs.

MOVING FORWARD WITH GLOBAL EDUCATION

There is no doubt that the fields of general and special education in the United States have benefited from global education (Collins & Zakariya, 1982). We cannot trace the history of these fields without recognizing their related foreign influences. In fact, even some of our teaching techniques have their origins from foreign countries. To a large measure, global education helps us to:

- learn about advancements among nations in many domains, including educational practices that we can use;

58   *Valuing Other Voices*

- form a better understanding of multiple ethnicities right here in the United States (i.e., the histories, languages, symbols, beliefs, values, and events that shape the lives of racially and culturally diverse students who are in the U.S. public schools);
- open doors of collaboration, consultation, and cooperation at sociopolitical, technological, and economic levels;
- reduce disruptions, disasters, and deaths that result from human and global crises;
- inform the majority (in this case, White Americans) about the contributions of minorities in the United States. For example, the U.S. Peace Corps program has provided Americans with the fascinating experiences of working in other countries with different sociocultural values; and
- be effective when working with immigrant children or refugees fleeing from violence or persecution to reside in the United States.

It is clear that global education is now a part of life. It is also clear that schools and institutions are redesigning their programs to reflect global realities. Since global education is becoming a reality in colleges and universities, it must be a graduation requirement for all general and special education programs. In colleges and universities and in most colleges/schools of education today, missions, visions, and goals are now highlighting global citizenship and perspectives. Honestly, we really do not have an option, if we are to live in a peaceful and harmonious world. Students and teachers must view themselves as important parts of the global village; and teacher educators must be world-minded and go beyond myopic perspectives in their thinking. In our works and pedagogical efforts, general educators, special educators, and related professionals must focus on:

- discussing the interconnectedness of the world's peoples, common issues, common purposes, and common solutions;
- fostering information on global collaboration in solving problems of disease, illiteracy, poverty, ethnic strife, terrorism, and poor utilization of the world's resources;
- conceptualizing justice, human rights, peace, and human relations on a global scale;
- using technology to enhance two-way communications among the world's children and youth and how expanding worldwide resources of the Internet can reach the remotest areas of the world;
- producing appropriate films of far and wide to reflect cultures, languages, beliefs, conditions, and contexts of people;

Global Learning and Teaching in General and Special Education   59

- enriching students' lives through interdisciplinary interactions with people from various countries who are a part of our local communities;
- exploring opportunities that are available in communities across the United States, particularly in human contacts and meaningful dialogues across cultures and national origins; and
- taking advantage of critical opportunities for linking with educators, related professionals, advocacy organizations, and many information sources that are available organizational websites and linkages.

CONCLUSION

As human beings, we must engage ourselves in "hearty" conversations that can foster our global collaborative, consultative, and cooperative spirits in general and special education (Obiakor, 2018). As educators, scholars, professionals, and leaders, it is time we started appreciating our roles as global citizens. We need leaders who value our world as one global entity. In addition, we must divorce ourselves from war-mongering myopically thinking leaders who use xenophobic hateful words like "shithole" to define other people and other countries. Frankly, all of us must focus on how we can resolve some of our burning global issues. We can no longer afford to operate in ignorance. As global citizens, we need each other; and as a result, we must learn from and about each other. We must continue to view education as a continuous process of growth; however, we do not need growth that is divorced from reality. We need growth that broadens the scope of our education and our humanity in measurable nonprejudicial ways.

CHAPTER 9

BUILDING SELF-CONCEPTS OF VULNERABLE CHILDREN AND YOUTH

Since we are not all perfect, we are vulnerable in some form or another. Real life problems affect real people, whether they are young, youthful, or old; and how they deal with it or how we deal with them matters (Holmes, 1994; Obiakor, 2018; Summers, 2004). Generally, we blame them for their plights and misgivings and urge them to pull themselves up by their own boot straps. In their strange response, they find safety in flight by giving up or by blaming the system for exposing them to unfortunate circumstances and situations. Sometimes, we tend to forget that many people do not have boots; and those who have boots may not have straps. Put another way, we fail to appreciate the fact that we are different interindividually and intraindividually and that we do not all handle crises in similar ways. Some people seem to be more devastated than others (Holmes, 1994; Obiakor, Mehring, & Schwenn, 1997). Earlier, in his book, *Life is Like a Lasting Storm*, Holmes (1994) acknowledged that:

In an ideal world, people would always benefit from a difficult situation and turn it to some personal gain. However, to categorically assume that a person will emerge renewed from a crisis is naïve and ignores the reality of what life crises can do to a person. I do not believe that every life crisis offers a challenge or an opportunity for positive growth experience, a chance to emerge a better and stronger person. In the real world, an event may leave a person changed in ways that could only be construed as diverse. A

Valuing Other Voices: Discourses That Matter in Education, Social Justice, and Multiculturalism, pp. 61–68
Copyright © 2020 by Information Age Publishing
All rights of reproduction in any form reserved.

62   *Valuing Other Voices*

person's failure to gain strength from such an event reflects the reality of personal experience, not some problem in the attitude or perspective of the person. (p. ix)

Holmes' (1994) statement above reveals why it is counterproductive and dangerous to blame or psychoanalyze people who confront life's crises and adversities. For example, many of our children and youth continue to experience overloads of blames from all sectors of our society even as they are exposed to disruptions, disasters, and deaths (Obiakor et al., 1997). The reality is that they do not deserve to be bombarded with voodoo theories, assumptions, and psychoanalyses—they need supports in reducing their vulnerabilities and in building their self-concepts and self-confidence to be successful in school and in life (see Obiakor et al., 1997). In addition, they need supports from their peers, parents, educational professionals, community entities, and government agencies. Such comprehensive supports will help ameliorate their problems and provide well-meaning strategies that will help them to maximize their fullest potential in whatever they decide to do (Harris, 2011; Obiakor, 2018). This idea is the central focus of this chapter.

WHO ARE VULNERABLE CHILDREN AND YOUTH?

In today's complex world, we are vulnerable human beings; and all children and youth are culpable to some form of vulnerabilities, especially when we consider the fact that recent terrorist acts leave no one safe anywhere in the world. In education specifically,

the term "vulnerable" is the current construct used to address students who are at risk of dropping out of school or of being mislabeled because of a myriad of socioeconomic, structural, educational, cultural, racial, linguistic, and societal burdens that impinge upon their learning and survival in school environments. (Beachum & Obiakor, 2018, p. vii)

Earlier, Mechanic and Tanner (2015) stated that "vulnerability results from developmental problems, personal incapacities, disadvantaged social status, inadequacy of interpersonal networks and supports, degraded neighborhoods and environments and the complex interactions of these factors over the life course" (p. 1220). Based on these explanations, one can conclude that vulnerable children and youth are people who continue to be disadvantaged, disenfranchised, and disillusioned as they interact with their environments at micro and macro levels. Going back to Holmes' (1994) perspective, these children and youth experience "life as a lasting storm." The critical question then is, How can we help them to build their self-concepts in the face of life's adversities and complexities so that they become functional people who can make functional goal-directed decisions.

It is common knowledge that our children and youth endure continuing threats to their normal development (Obiakor, 1990, 1992a, 1992b). As Shoaf (1990) noted more than 2 decades ago, "many children today struggle to cope with a world more uncertain and more frightening than ever before" (p. 13). Some of their problems include:

- prevalence of single-parent families of families without father figures;
- alarming rate of child abuse and neglect;
- unending economic and social pressures on parents;
- rampancy of drug abuse and dealing;
- poor nutrition as a result of poverty;
- preponderance of teenage pregnancy or "babies" having babies;
- disturbing rates of misery and suicide;
- alarming rate of diverse or family breakdown;
- unnecessary selfishness or the "me-first" syndrome;
- self-concept misinterpretations;
- myth of socioeconomic dissonance; and
- negative perception of the less fortunate, disadvantaged, and helpless individuals as socioeconomic liabilities.

SELF-CONCEPT AS A CONSTRUCT: CONCEPTUALIZATIONS

The "self" plays a critical role in the uplift of human beings, especially when it comes to our children and youth. How we view the self and how we interact with ourselves and other people's selves are critical in dealing with life's circumstances and situations. To a large measure, self-concept is an important educational phenomenon; and as a result, it is prone to myriad explanations and interpretations, some "perceptual" and others "operational."

Perceptual Model of Self-Concept

The perceptual model of self-concept is traditional in nature and sees self-concept as an interrelated perception of the self. Based on this model, self-concept and survival in life are positively correlated. This

64 *Valuing Other Voices*

means that a child who feels good about himself or herself usually succeeds in school programs and in life (Canfield & Siccone, 1993; Canfield & Wells, 1976; Purkey, 1970; Siconne & Canfield, 1993; Snygg & Combs, 1949). Although this notion has dominated the literature, the definition, evaluation, and interpretation of self-concept have attracted varying conceptualizations. For example, the traditional conceptualization of self-concept describes how one sees or perceives himself/herself. In addition, In addition, this conceptualization assumes that self-perceptions are fully developed before children and youth enter the classroom or come to school for the first time. As Canfield and Wells (1976) pointed out,

> by the time a child reaches school age his [her] self-concept is well formed and his [her] reactions to learning, to school failure and success and to physical, social and emotional climate of the classroom will be determined by the beliefs and attitudes he [she] has about himself [herself]. (p. 3)

Based on the aforementioned conceptualization, a change in self-concepts is likely to affect a wide range of behaviors. In other words, when one aspect of the child's or youth's self-concept is affected, there is a ripple effect on his or her entire self-concept. This means that the teacher can make judgments about the student's school life and home life—this puts the teacher or professional in a precarious position of investing time in situations that are outside his/her domain. When educational professionals go beyond their scope of duty and begin to think that they know everything, they begin to label and categorize students making it difficult to design Individualized Education Plans, especially for those who have special needs.

It is important to note that traditional instruments that measure self-concept have failed to define self-concept explicitly. So, even when they reliably produce consistent results, they do not measure what they purport to measure because of their lack of validity. As a result, they lack operational and quantifiable clarity (Harris, 2011; Obiakor & Algozzine, 1995b; Summers, 2004). For example, the questions in these instruments are arranged area specifically and they are interpreted globally. Problems and contradictions emerge when specific strengths and weaknesses are globalized as "positive" or "negative." Two important questions come to mind. How do we as professionals respond to interventions or design intervention and remediation programs when we cannot area-specifically identify the strengths and weaknesses of children and youth who are already vulnerable? To help vulnerable children and youth to maximize their fullest potential, should we not go beyond perceptions and labels to discover their specific likes, dislikes, strengths, weaknesses, interests, and disinterests, to mention a few?

Operational Model of Self-Concept

The operational model of self-concept is the alternative contemporary explanation of self-concept. This model conceptualizes self-concept as an individual's repertoire of self-descriptive behavior (Muller, 1978; Muller, Chambliss, & Muller, 1982). This means that self-concept has some multi-dimensionality and functionality attached to its definition, description, and interpretation (Harris, 2011; Helper, 1955; Marsh, Parker, & Barnes, 1985; Marsh & Smith, 1986; Obiakor, 1992b, 2001, 2008; Shavelson, Bolus, & Keasling, 1980; Summers, 2004). Based on this framework, a vulnerable child's self-descriptions can be accurate or inaccurate, consistent or contradictory, extensive or limited, and covert or overt; and they may sometimes change as contexts change.

As indicated, from a contemporary perspective, self-concept is quantifiable and multidimensional. Muller et al. (1982) contended that self-concept has three subsets (self-knowledge, self-esteem, and self-ideal), which can be measured in the areas of physical maturity, peer relations, academic success, and school adaptiveness. Specifically, self-knowledge explains a person's knowledge of himself/herself. Self-esteem explains self-love or self-valuation. And, self-ideal explains a person's willingness to expend efforts to achieve his/her goals. A logical extension is that a person might know himself/herself without loving himself/herself; and a person might love himself/herself without the willingness to work hard to achieve his/her goal. These collectively mean that dividing the self-concept of vulnerable children and youth into discrete construct areas has several educational implications. As Muller et al. (1982) noted,

> Instructional strategies designed to alter self-concept can be focused on those aspects of self-concept directly relevant to the school.... This eliminates the need to intrude into the personal or family aspects of the student's life. A related implication is that programs designed to impact self-concept in one area (e.g., peer relations) are not likely to impact self in other areas (e.g., academics). Our work has convinced us that for the majority of students, effective classroom management of self-concept can be accomplished by limiting our efforts to the school life of the child. (p. 9)

To a large extent, Marshall (1989) concurred with the multidimensionality of self-concept and exposed the impact of cultural differences on the assessment and instruction of students on self-concept domains. She remarked that "the importance of each of these domains differs for individuals and families, and among cultures. A low self-evaluation in one domain, such as athletic ability, may have little effect on the individual if it is not considered important in a particular family of culture" (Marshall,

66 *Valuing Other Voices*

1989, p. 45). Clearly, Marshall's (1989) statement confirmed the inherent biases and prejudices in self-concept assessment tools and interpretations.

BUILDING SELF-CONCEPTS OF VULNERABLE LEARNERS

It is common knowledge that the self is an important part of the person; and this self cannot be divorced from the development of our humanity. Santrock and Yussen (1989) agreed that the self is the core of a child's growth and development. As a result, vulnerable children and youth must be helped to build their self-concepts, especially when one considers their multidimensional problems in school and in life. For example, the simplistic view that people should pull themselves up by their own boot straps must stop. In addition, viewing self-descriptions as positive or negative based on majority values is self-destructive. To assess self-concepts, we need instruments that define and measure the constructs that they purport to measure (Harris, 2011; Obiakor & Algozzine, 1995a; Obiakor & Stile, 1990; Summers, 2004). And, in our interpretation of results, we must be area specific and avoid globalizing human behaviors (Obiakor, 2018).

As educational professionals, we must understand who vulnerable children and youth are—this will prevent us from solving problems that do not exist. We must be client-centered as we work with children and youth; however, we must be quantifiable in our identification, assessment, categorization, placement, and instruction. In addition, we must be behavioral and observable in our intervention approaches. It is important that we design individualized education programs to specifically address and solve the areas of self-concept that show some weakness. Finally, we must acknowledge that "low" self-concept in one area may not lead to "low" self-concepts in other areas; and culturally, what is acceptable in one situation or circumstance may not be acceptable in other situations.

To build self-concepts of vulnerable children and youth, we must be willing to shift our traditional paradigm on self-concept. We must realize that self-concept is not a static phenomenon that is genetically handed-down. It can be changed and enhanced through effective interventions (Obiakor, 1992b, 2008). In addition, it can be observed, described, measured, and developed. Such a conceptualization can reduce self-fulfilling prophesies that force vulnerable children and youth to be victims or be viewed as victims. Put another way, it is counterproductive to globalize their behaviors as "positive" or "negative." Like other human beings, they are capable of learning and growing; and they are capable of making mistakes. We must create opportunities for them they experience novel and dynamic situations.

Building Self-Concepts of Vulnerable Children and Youth   67

Since self-concept must not be based on perceptions, we must be operational in helping vulnerable children and youth to make functional goal-directed decisions. As a consequence, we must:

- care for children and youth with special needs;
- have reasonable expectations when working with children and youth;
- listen to vulnerable children and youth;
- involve children and youth in action-oriented activities;
- generate general praise for measurable activities;
- praise the obvious—the obvious is sometimes ignored by close-minded professionals;
- use peer teaching to improve self-worth of children and youth;
- emphasize positives without being patronizing;
- help vulnerable children and youth to recognize their strengths;
- inform vulnerable children and youth that it is okay to make mistakes and that no one is perfect;
- expose vulnerable children and youth to productive leaders and leadership skills;
- provide children and youth with realistic mentors who can also serve as role models; and
- expose vulnerable children and youth to creative and educational adventures.

CONCLUSION

Self-concept is an important educational phenomenon; and the self is inextricably tied to the human being. We cannot divorce the self from the person. For vulnerable children and youth who confront divergent problems that range from abuse and neglect to frightening uncertainty about their future, educators and related professionals must look for ways to enhance their self-understanding, self-valuation, and self-responsibility. They deserve to be treated fairly like other human beings—discounting their existence or the plights that confront them with baseless assumptions, perceptions, and generalizations are counterproductive.

As a construct, self-concept is viewed from different perspectives. Some people view it simplistically as one feels about himself/herself. This perceptual view sees self-concept is an interrelated perception of the self (i.e., what happens in one area of the self affects other areas of the self). In other ways, a person who loves himself/herself always works hard to

68 *Valuing Other Voices*

achieve his/her goals. Even though this assumption is traditional, it is a fallacy that does not make common or educational sense. It narrowly globalizes both strengths and weaknesses as either "positive" or "negative." Of late, educators and related professionals have been looking for innovative ways to reach all learners, especially those children and youth who are vulnerable. One of those ways is the response to intervention, an intervention model that forces professionals to be area specific in designing individualized programs. Viewing self-concept as a self-descriptive behavior that can change as contexts change and that can be observed, quantified, measured, and interpreted values the specific strengths and weaknesses that students bring to school. This view inspires professionals to focus on school contexts instead of engaging in generalizations that are prejudicial to students and educational professionals. In addition, this opens multidimensional doors to build self-concepts of vulnerable children and youth.

To build self-concepts of vulnerable learners, it is critical that we interpret self-concepts area-specifically and situation-specifically since our behaviors and reactions change as situations change. I believe we must care for our students and involve them in the caring process. In addition, we must have realistic expectations of our students. It is dangerous to have unwarranted "high" of "low" expectations that can lead to self-fulfilling prophecies and unwarranted frustrations that can additionally lead to school drop-outs, achievement gaps, drug dealing and abuse, "Babies" having babies, high suicide rates, and jail times. The statement, "failure is not an option" is unrealistic—failure can build self-knowledge and self-ideal. Clearly, a failure is not the "be all and end all" of any human being; and a failure in one situation might not lead to failures in other situations. As educational professionals, our goal must be to help vulnerable children and youth to build their self-concepts while maximizing their potential, recognizing their strengths and weaknesses, emphasizing their positives, using their peers to mentor them, and praising the obvious without patronizing them. As Holmes (1994) finally concluded,

> To efficiently address a temporal real-life problem, the person experiencing the problem and those who are trying to help must deal with the reality of what the person is experiencing. Neither the person nor the helper should approach to resolve distress as if the origin of the problem were psychopathological. It is not. Moreover, life situations outside the person's control may change, the person may learn new ways to cope, or the person may learn ways to change the situation itself. Thus, the possibility of change offers hope of eventual resolution of the problem. Nonetheless, the distress must be endured, and the person's efforts to cope with that distress require support. (p. 4)

CHAPTER 10

BENEFITS OF EDUCATING AND HIRING AN "AFRICAN" IN AMERICA'S HIGHER EDUCATION

This chapter tells my personal story as an "African" journeying through America's colleges and universities. It is based on my personal experiences and not the personal experiences of *all* Africans. Based on my interactions with Africans in higher education, I have seen and heard of similar experiences with just a few variations (Obiakor, 2002; Obiakor& Gordon, 2003; Obiakor & Grant, 2005; Obiakor, Grant, & Obi, 2010). As a personal research venture, I went through "rate my professor" of many professors of African origin. Coincidentally, I found that the comments were almost similar for these professors, especially those in colleges/ schools of education. In addition, I have seen and heard of similar tenure and promotion stories of these professors despite their teaching abilities, research interests, scholarly endeavors, and professional leaderships (Obiakor et al., 2010; Obiakor & Grant, 2005). In most cases, there were frantic efforts to look for areas of weaknesses of these professors to deflate their capabilities and downplay their achievements. Sadly, excuses are used and invented by tenure and promotion committees and college leaders to discontinue or let go of these fine professionals in their chosen professions (Obiakor & Gordon, 2003). Instead of devaluing their achievements, the voices of Africans should be heard as teachers, scholars,

---

Valuing Other Voices: Discourses That Matter in Education, Social Justice, and Multiculturalism, pp. 69–87
Copyright © 2020 by Information Age Publishing
All rights of reproduction in any form reserved.

70   *Valuing Other Voices*

professionals, and leaders. In this chapter, I let the cat out of the bag so that newcomers to higher education will learn the ways the games are played and find solutions very early to build successful careers. In addition, using my personal experiences, I debunk the myths that Africa and Africans have not been beneficial to the United States.

I know that using the word "African" tells only a part of the story. Being an African does not fully define or expose what it means to be a Nigerian, Kenyan, South African, Libyan, Senegalese, Liberian, Ugandan, or an Ethiopian, Egyptian, Algerian, to mention a few. Using the word, "African" also plays into a dangerous generalization that lends itself to illusory presumptions and conclusions. There is no easy way to discuss the construct, African. Since my goal is to improve social justice, human valuing, and multiculturalism, I do believe we are all different intra-individually and inter-individually. I feel uncomfortable talking about Africa in the way xenophobes, racists, and narrow-minded people represent it. A good example is the remark by the 45th president of the United States, Donald Trump who referred to African countries as "shit-hole" countries. Narrow-minded individuals such as Trump view, define, and treat Africa as a village or country even though it is a powerful continent with powerful independent countries, peoples, natural resources, languages, and cultures.

Additionally, adding the word, "benefits" to the title of this chapter is tricky and pushes the envelope. To many xenophobes and racists, Africa and Africans are of no use to the United States and bring nothing to the table. That is why Trump's statement about Africans coming from "shithole" countries is close-minded and disgraceful and did not surprise many of us. He just happened to reiterate what many Americans think, as evidenced in their books, movies, and actions, to mention a few. It is no surprise that I continue to be asked very offensive questions such as "How did you come into the United States? Do you have roads in Africa? Do you have houses in Africa? When did you start to speak English? Where did you learn to dress fashionably like you do? How many wives do you have? Have you ever killed a lion with your bare hands? Do you drink blood? Are Africans cannibals who eat fellow humans? When and why did you come to the United States?" The remarkable irony is that Africans have historically come to the United States. In fact, those who were brought here as slaves built the United States and have always put their lives on the line to defend it. For example, while they we were viewed as sub-humans in those days, they fought and died during the United States' civil war. These Africans now known as African Americans have continued to contribute measurably and remarkably to the well-being and success of the United States at all levels.

Recognizing our differences as human beings is an absolute necessity (Obiakor, 2001b, 2008, 2018). No doubt, we perceive differently, learn differently, and consume information differently. However, as human beings, we learn from actions; we learn from mistakes; we learn from experiences; and we learn from trials and tribulations (Dewey, 1958). For me, I learned and did a lot as a student, professor, scholar, professional, and leader in America's higher education. Sometimes, I laughed; sometimes, I cried; and sometimes, I was emotionless. My experiences have been varied; and I learned from all of them. These experiences have made me better, more spiritual, and more multicultural. I now know what it means to be disadvantaged, disenfranchised, and disillusioned. In fact, I now know what it means to be a vulnerable stranger in a strange land. To a large measure, rather than learn to become a victim, I have learned what it takes to be more resilient and successful.

The obvious benefits of being an African in America's higher education appear to be getting the opportunity to be educated by others and getting the opportunity to educate others. But, they are not as simple as that! Emigrating from Nigeria to be educated in America was not easy—it was emotionally, psychologically, and financially costly. And, as a professor in America's higher education, it has been an emotional roller-coaster, sometimes high and sometimes low. Put another way, like other Blacks and immigrants, my experiences have been sometimes joyful and sometimes vexing (Obiakor, 2018). And, I can now say that I came, I saw; but with pains and scars, I continue to learn!

COMING TO AMERICA

The movie *Coming to America* (Paramount Pictures, 1988) was a fictional comedy that starred Eddie Murphy in the lead role. In this movie, the much pampered young African prince came to Queens, New York to find himself an American wife. To achieve his goal, he mopped floors, lived in rat-infested apartments, disguised and hid his real identity, went through changes, and met a lady who later became his wife in the African nation of Zamunda. To many Africans who come to the United States for new lives, the experiences are real and not fictitious. Most of them go through changes, live in very "poor" areas of the town while trying to raise their children and survive the brutal realities of bigotry, racism, disadvantages, disenfranchisement, and disillusionment. In the midst of these predicaments, they still remember the family and cultural obligations of their home countries and dedicatedly survive against the odds in a strange land that sometimes appears unwelcoming.

Before I left Nigeria for the United States, my parents advised me to fear no one, respect everyone, and treat people with dignity. Being a strict Catholic, my father told me to respect my brand and treat others as I

72   *Valuing Other Voices*

would like to be treated (Obiakor, 2008). I was emotionally drained to leave my family for a strange land. I boarded my plane in Lagos, Nigeria to come to the United States to pursue a master's degree in special education at Texas Christian University (TCU), I never knew what my later experiences would be. I left everything as my mother would say, "in the hands of God." When my plane landed at John F. Kennedy Airport, I got out of the plane to take a taxi to New York LaGuardia Airport. I remembered that taxis have to be full to move. So, when I saw three White men in the taxi, I thought that the taxi was ready to move; and I got in. That was a mistake! On our way to LaGuardia Airport, the taxi stopped next to a river. I did not know that those three White men were criminals and marauders. Under gun point, they took my traveler's checks worth lots of money. I was scared that they were going to kill me! I still remember that one of them was seriously asthmatic—his eyes were red as he blew his inhaler. As they took my checks, one of them slapped me in a paternalistic manner and said, "Good boy." They dropped me off at LaGuardia Airport, allowed me to carry my two briefcases, and drove off.

When I arrived at LaGuardia Airport, I found out that I missed my flight to the Dallas/Fort Worth Airport. The people who worked at the booking counter were nice, caring, and sensitive—they put me in another plane and we landed in Dallas. As directed, I took a bus to the campus. The next day, I met with the director of international student affairs who already heard about my experiences. Since my tuition was already paid, I did not feel so stressed about not having any money. The director and I made arrangements to keep my negative experiences confidential and private out of the public domain. I was offered a job on campus—I was so happy and thankful for his sensitivity and humanity. For years, I never shared these experiences with anyone, including my parents and family members. What were the lessons here? I learned so much about my resiliency level, especially when my vulnerability was tested. This resiliency level has been exposed in my teaching, scholarship, professional, and leadership activities; and my students and colleagues have tried to emulate it.

STUDYING IN AMERICA

Based on what I read and the pictures in the catalog, I thought that TCU had many Black students. That was not the case when I arrived at the campus! I knew that TCU was a good university; however, I was unaware of its powerful reputation in Texas and the United States as a whole. I knew that I would work hard to excel academically; but, I never could imagine the kind of questions that I would be answering. While I was

Benefits of Educating and Hiring an "African" in America's Higher Education 73

learning in class and trying to understand cultures and values of the people of the United States, I was also educating my peers, classmates, and professors. In one of my classes, one of the professors asked me, "Why are you so smart about global issues. You seem to be way ahead of your peers." This statement happened when one of my classmates talked about the greatness of America and how it did not need help from other countries. I asked him if he knew where America got its oil for its industries. I wanted to know if this student knew about Nigeria's contribution to the United States. None of my classmates knew! After this class discussion, I gained new friends in my program that same day—my classmates benefited from my academic and global knowledge.

In another situation, a beautiful White TCU female student approached me and told me that she admired my sense of class and fashion and that she would like to date me. After hesitating for a while, I told her that I was ready to give it a trial. She planned a date and told me that she would take me to Fort Worth zoo. I found this to be very strange, but accepted. When we got to the zoo, she told me that she knew that I was going to like the date since I came from Africa where we lived and played with all kinds of wild animals. Though I appreciated the gesture, I was shocked! I told her that I was born and raised in a big city and that I had never seen such animals in my life. She was shocked and acknowledged that I was saying was not reflected in the news, books, or movies. She apologized and actually fell in love with me; however, I was focused on my education and not ready for any deep relationship. This beautiful kind lady learned a lot from me; and I am sure that her life was changed by interacting with me. Funny enough, I had similar romantic experiences with ladies from different cultural backgrounds like the ones that I had with that beautiful wonderful lady.

As a student at TCU, I wanted to keep myself occupied—I was told by my father that "an idle mind is the devil's work place." The result is that I applied for and got two job offers; one as a dish washer in a fish restaurant and the other as someone who fries tacos at Taco Bell. I was not experienced in performing those types of work. I was slow and sluggish in performing my duties. Most of my coworkers were students; and they never knew that I was also a student. I was glad to see and learn their work habits. My supervisors were high school graduates and college dropouts—they were rude, crude, and unrefined in the ways that they talked to employees. I felt very awkward and out of place in these situations. Consequently, I applied for and got a job at *Fort Worth Star Telegram* to work in the Associated Press Room. In this job, I collected the news as they came and forwarded them to the desks of respective editors (e.g., music editor). I worked from midnight to 8:00 A.M. Many of the workers did not even say hello to me; however, the managing editor stopped by almost every day to

74 *Valuing Other Voices*

say hello to me. At one point, he told me: "I am Jewish. I am proud of your determination. Some people want me to fire you because of your lateness; but, I will not. Festus, I offered this job to you because you are the only one among the applicants who said that you will use the money that you earn to pursue your PhD degree. I will support you any way I can." I was pleasantly shocked that he looked my way and even talked to me. I never missed a day of work; however, I was sometimes late for work when I overslept. Surprisingly, this managing editor refused to fire me. The simple but fantastic message here is that, "All White people are not hateful and racist."

By November 1981, I gained admission to pursue my PhD degree at New Mexico State University, Las Cruces, New Mexico. I continued to work at the *Fort Worth Star Telegram* until August 1982 when I drove in my new, red Ford Escort to Las Cruces, New Mexico. I never knew if I was traveling on the right track, but was convinced that I was following the map's directions when I saw, "Welcome to El Paso, Texas!" I was told at the gas station that I was almost in Las Cruces, New Mexico—it was a joyful feeling that I was not lost. For the first few nights, I slept in my car. Before long, I met a guy from my tribe in Nigeria who was working on his master's degree in engineering. He allowed him to live with him for a few months before I found an apartment in El Paso, Texas where I landed a job at *El Paso Times*. This job was very stressful. I was fortunate to get some of graduate assistantship. One particular full professor was consistently harassing me—each time, he walked past me, he noted: "We believe in quality hear!" This was unnerving to me to the extent that I began to avoid this man! To my greatest surprise, the Dean of the College of Education, Dr. David Byrne invited me for a meeting in his office. Though I was doing well in my program, I was worried that I had done something wrong. During the meeting, the dean asked the professor, "Why do you consistently tell Festus that we believe in quality here?" The professor was shocked and could not come up with an answer. The dean warned him to desist from doing that again; and he informed this professor to locate a good graduate assistantship for me in the department. I never knew how the dean knew about my traumatic harassment. This is still amazing to me.

As a student at New Mexico State University, I experienced many caring professors—through their actions, they wanted me to be successful in all my endeavors. However, I endured misperceptions, negative presumptions, and blatantly hateful behaviors. I was forced to dig deep in my soul to survive. For instance, some professors would give me a B+ instead of an A without clear reasons. One of them actually said, "B+ grade is not bad for a Black student" and that I should have been happy. One of them would always remind me that he never understood one word that I said

Benefits of Educating and Hiring an "African" in America's Higher Education   75

because of my accent. And, one of them would always tell me: "That's not how we behave in America." In fact, one of them would always tell me to dress down to give the impression that I was a serious student—he told me that I was so clean, that I wore expensive and classy suits, and that I smelled too good. There are many more examples of inhumane treatments that I received—these experiences made me smarter, stronger, and more determined to be successful in school and to make my mark in life. In spite of these negative experiences, I earned another master's degree in psychology (instructional psychology) in August 1986 and a PhD in special education (curriculum and instruction) and a minor in educational administration in December 1986. In the end, I was amazed at the level of ignorance of some of my college professors and peers. These individuals were smart academically, but not-so-smart about life and the world in which we live. Rather than teach me, they were learning from me. It was wonderful to teach my professors and peers about the world outside their world.

As a student, I frequently visited and spent some time in the university's Black Program. The director was a unique advocate of Black students on campus; and I respected him for that. I wanted to bridge the relational gaps between Africans and African American students on campus; and the director appreciated and supported me. During this period, I visited the Black Program to see the director. There, I saw two beautiful female students—I found out that they are Jamaicans and twins; and fortunately, one of them is now my wife of over 35 years with four wonderful children who are succeeding in their respective endeavors. For sure, if I did not come to the United States, I would not have met my wife and we would not have had our children.

TEACHING COLLEGE STUDENTS IN AMERICA

As a graduate assistant at New Mexico State University, I helped in doing assigned projects and taught an introduction to special education class as an instructor. I grew a lot during this process; and my experiences were eye-opening, good, and sometimes bad. I was fortunate to have the opportunity, since my academic advisor was personally involved in the process. He gave me good feedback. When I was calm and jovial, the students complained; and when I was strict and tough, they complained. In my class, I had a few Latino students, majority White students, and no Black student. I wanted students' feedbacks to be based on course content. Surprisingly, their feedbacks were based on my accent, how I dressed, how I laughed, how real or unreal I was, and so on. I never knew that my skin color and race could influence how they felt about me as a

76 *Valuing Other Voices*

teacher. In the end, I was pleased that most of my students rated me highly as a great teacher. My advisor gave me a wonderful advice when he said: "Be you. As long as you have given it your best, that's what counts!" It was strange when I saw that my White peers were buying pizza and gifts for their students at the end of every semester. When I asked why they did that, they told me, "Festus, you have to play the game. It is not about quality. We were advised to do this to get good evaluations." In my professional career, I refused to play this game despite the odds against me.

After graduating with my PhD degree, I was surprised that my White peers who I helped to read and write their dissertations got job offers immediately to teach in colleges and universities. For me, interviewing for and getting job offers were difficult and strange—I interviewed for jobs in many colleges and universities and my experiences were negatively shocking. I was asked weird questions that sometimes were demeaning and against the law; and I tried very hard to be composed and emotionally intelligent. Two offers (one from Frostburg State University, Frostburg, Maryland and the other from Rust College, Holly Springs, Mississippi) appeared to be good fits to me—it was difficult for me to make a choice because I liked both opportunities. Frostburg State University was enticing because it was going to give me the opportunity to work with the Student Support Services Program. And, Rust College (RC) was going to give me the opportunity to work at a historically Black college/university. Frostburg State University offered me a salary of $23,000; and RC offered me $16,000. Interestingly, I chose to go to RC, an opportunity that I still value today.

Teaching at RC as an assistant professor was a dream job; however, it had its trials and tribulations. Though I a Black teaching in a predominant Black college, I was still a stranger in a strange land. I was a foreigner whose forefathers sold his brothers and sisters—that was a mortal sin to me because I could not understand the wisdom or good rationale for engaging in such a devastating historical action. However, I did find that many Africans were given the opportunity to maximize their fullest potential. In fact, at RC and many Black colleges, we have had African immigrants as vice presidents or even presidents. By the same token, people of Indian and Asiatic origins have fared well in historically Black colleges/universities. Sadly, they are still viewed as "model minorities" by African Americans. At RC, I started a television show, "New Dimensions" that focused on research done by faculty members. Additionally, I initiated a refereed journal that had regional and national visibilities. As a teacher, I was active and productive—my goal was to help students to pass the National Teachers Examination. I had a deal with the academic dean where he would put $5,000 in my travel budget if I was able to raise the passing scores of students. I told him that I would raise the scores if I was

Benefits of Educating and Hiring an "African" in America's Higher Education   77

allowed to teach four courses: Introduction to Education, Introduction to Special Education, Human Growth and Development, and Measurement and Evaluation. I taught these classes and spent time mentoring and working with students—the result was remarkable as many students (including the current superintendent of Holly Springs School District) passed the National Teachers Examination; and I got my $5,000 travel budget. Two remarkable life-changing things happened to my life at RC—my son was born; and this changed my perspective about life. Also, I pledged as a member of Omega Psi Phi Fraternity—this brought me closer to my brothers. It became clear to me that in life "many are called, but only a few are chosen." Since then, I have added my fraternity's cardinal principles (*Manhood, Scholarship, Perseverance, and Uplift*) to my modus vivendi.

I left RC for the University of Tennessee at Chattanooga (UTC) where I was the first African American faculty in my department. I experienced the worst racism and discrimination of my life. Consider the following examples:

- A White, female colleague had the consistent behavior of reminding me to go to a speech and language pathologist to work on my accent. Ironically, I helped this colleague to read and edit her papers for conference presentations and her manuscript for readiness for publication. On one occasion, she wanted me to read and edit her manuscript and I responded: "I will not have to read your manuscript today because I am on way to a speech and language pathologist." Funny enough, she did not get the joke.

- On another occasion, I came to my office and saw a picture of a man hanging from a tree. That was scary; however, one White male colleague thought that it was funny.

- Some students came to my office and told me that they were told to tape my classes.

- My student evaluations never reflected instructional feedbacks— they were always about unrelated issues (e.g., the jokes that I told, the examples that I gave, my discussions about caring and cultural responsiveness, etc.).

- On one occasion, I saw the provost of the university and greeted, "Good morning, Dr. P.;" and she responded: "What makes this a good morning."

Despite the aforementioned problems, I was fortunate to meet Drs. Rod Fowler and Loretta Prater. Rod took me under his wing, mentored me, and supported me as a human being. He changed my perspectives on

78 *Valuing Other Voices*

"Whiteness" and race; and he was consistently kind to me. Loretta was also an amazing woman who invited my wife and me to church on Sundays and to parties at her house regularly. She was a distinguished beautiful woman who had impeccable integrity—we both wrote the popular "Each One Reach One" Program that was funded by the Tennessee Department of Education and focused on recruiting, retaining, and graduating Black males to work in elementary schools. Interestingly, some of these men are now school leaders in Tennessee and around the nation. In the end, two remarkable things happened to me—my wife and I had our two daughters—they totally changed my life and have grown to be ladies of distinction.

From UTC, I went to Henderson State University as an associate professor and my stay there was brief because my wife was not offered a job as was promised. At Henderson State University, a colleague and I wrote the "Reach One Male Educator" Program that was funded by the Arkansas Department of Education and focused on recruiting, retaining, and graduating males into elementary schools. In addition, I was the guest editor (with Dr. Bridgie Alexis Ford, University of Akron and Dr. James M. Patton, College of William & Mary) of a special issue of *Exceptional Children*, the top research journal in the field of special education—the special issue focused for the first time on African Americans with exceptionalities). Despite these remarkable and historical achievements, I had similar negative experiences as those at UTC in less blatant ways. In the end, at Henderson State University, I was fortunate to meet Dr. Charles Weiner, a head of another department in the college of education. He was an intellectual human being who also taught me about valuing "Whiteness" and the beauties of caring and sensitivity. Not long ago, I met Charles again as a retired colleague when I interviewed for the associate dean position of the College of Education at Henderson State University. Though I was not offered the job, it was a great opportunity to wine and dine with Charles and his wife as destiny would have it.

I accepted a job offer as an associate professor at Emporia State University (ESU), Emporia, Kansas. Emporia was a small city that afforded me a very progressive livelihood. At ESU, I worked hard to beef up my stock as a teacher, scholar, professional, and leader. Before long, I began to coordinate all the special education programs in out department, teach new and interesting courses (e.g., social psychology and multicultural psychology) and develop very strong relationships with my colleagues who turned to be successful leaders and professionals. For example, the department chair rose to be the dean of the graduate school and the vice president for academic affairs and later the president of Dalton State College in Georgia. He was replaced by another department chair who is the current dean of the Teachers College. The then dean of the Teachers

Benefits of Educating and Hiring an "African" in America's Higher Education 79

College became the provost and vice president for academic affairs. Another colleague went to a state university in Virginia where he later became the associate dean of the college of education; and he left there for a private university where he became the dean of the college of Education and got promoted to be the assistant to the vice president. All these colleagues were not just teachers and scholars; they were also leaders. I enjoyed my stay at ESU—it was a very productive period of my career. For example, I became a tenured Full Professor at ESU. However, other professors who were less productive were getting distinguished professor awards; and I found this to be unfair and racist. As a consequence, I had to leave ESU because of the blatant racist and intimidating leadership tactic of the president, the first female president of a university in the state of Kansas.

I left ESU to accept a senior scholar position in the College of Education at the University of Wisconsin-Milwaukee (UWM). Because of the lack of minority faculty in the Department of Exceptional Education, I was put in that department as a tenured full professor. I had no computer or phone in my new office—it seemed to be a setup to fail. The department was negative, corrosive, and dangerous; and every effort was made to make my life in the department a living hell. I was reminded of the aforementioned problems that I encountered when I was at UTC. Not surprisingly, all the problems that I encountered at UTC manifested themselves in much more intensive fashion at UWM. Though UWM professed to be the premier urban university for the State of Wisconsin, it was the most racist, xenophobic, close-minded, and jealous infested place that I have ever worked at. Specifically, minority faculty and staff members were jealous of each other; they never respected each other; and they found it difficult to collaborate, consult, and cooperate with each other. All of these made it easy for the majority to destroy whoever they wanted to target with the cooperation of minority faculty or staff. It was a very strange environment where the underlying goals were to dishonor excellence and hard work and silence any strong civil rights advocate or voice on campus. It was a well-organized systemic plot to destroy anyone who does not follow the majority rules. It was like a plantation where the slave master had all the power with a few "sold-out" informants—it was unbelievably shameless! Since I became known as a renowned teacher, scholar, professional, and leader, jealousy toward me intensified creating a scary "dog-eat-dog" environment. Good leadership was lacking at the deanship, provost, and chancellor levels at UWM. For example, the chancellor was a Latino; but, he was useless on issues related to discrimination, racism, and xenophobia. Even though we had an African American dean of the College of Education, the college was not caring or welcoming to those voices who questioned incompetent leadership. Why should we be

80 Valuing Other Voices

surprised? This dean told me that he had never been to any part of Africa in his life—he was truly a racist tool and xenophobe who hated Africa and Africans based on his actions. The important lesson for me at UWM is that just being a Latino, an African American, or a minority does not mean that someone cannot be ignorant, racist, or xenophobic.

LEADING A DEPARTMENT OR DIVISION

I began thinking about leadership at ESU when I began to coordinate six special education programs. I remember writing 18 folios for my programs during one State and national accreditation visits. I helped to streamline our programs and make our programs marketable. I learned a lot from these leadership experiences. Coming to UWM was not as fruitful as I had hoped. The stressful environment at UWM began to convince me that leadership matters in higher education and in life. All societal ills are caused by the lack of leadership. As a result, I began to flirt with the idea of becoming a department or college leader. I suggested that we rotate leadership in my department. Yes, my White colleagues were sharing and rotating the leadership with each other by voting each other into power. They believed it was their God-given right to run the department any way they wanted. When it came to yearly evaluations they suggested *no* meritocracy in rewarding faculty productivity because majority of them were lazy and contributed nothing to the department. I questioned all of these unfortunate and bigoted interactions and transactions. They refused to rotate departmental leadership and voted for each other consistently. The politics was dirty! I advocated for hiring faculty and staff who come from culturally and linguistically diverse (CLD) backgrounds. There were positive moves in recruiting CLD faculty and staff; however, the "powers that be" made sure that these individuals were submissive—the game of "divide and conquer" was in full operation. In the midst of the turmoil, there was an opportunity for associate dean position in the college of education. I was among the top two candidates. The less experienced African American female faculty who I gave publication opportunities in my department was hired by the African American male dean. The blatant exhibition of hatred and xenophobia was there; and my spirit of justice was shattered. Interestingly, the African American female associate dean has since become a dean in two major research universities. *All things being equal, if I had the opportunity, my leadership career would have been propelled also.*

As the years went by at UWM, I ran for the coordinator of graduate programs for the department. Our graduate programs were bleeding to death—there were just a handful of students who came from CLD back-

Benefits of Educating and Hiring an "African" in America's Higher Education 81

grounds—I wanted these numbers to be increased. To my greatest surprise, I was voted to serve as the coordinator of graduate program. I represented the department and college very well on graduate-related issues and helped to market our programs locally, regionally, nationally, and internationally. On a couple of occasions, I served as acting chair of the department when the chair is out of town. I began my job search as a dean of a college/school of Education. I had many telephone, Skype, and Zoom interviews. In addition, I have many campus invitations and visits and was unsuccessful in landing a deanship position. I came close to landing some deanship jobs; but, that was not enough! As a result, I had to go with "Plan B"—that was becoming a department head or chair—this plan worked.

I left UWM for The City College of New York (CCNY) to serve as department chair. Before now, I had visited New York for conferences, but never lived in it. It was fascinating to live in Harlem New York—I lived in the same apartment complex with former Governor Patterson of New York and the United States Congressman Rangel. Ironically, right next to this expensive complex was a huge housing project. Our school of education was led by a Latina interim dean. She was culturally aware of whom she was; however, that was not reflected in her leadership style and actions—this could be translated as either good or bad. For example, when she hired me, she told me that tenure would be easy and that CCNY never offered tenure to department chairs immediately; and that was lie. I met another chair from another school who told me that he came to CCNY with tenure and promotion. Even though she was consistently disrespected by the majority White faculty members, she downplayed that and gave them so much power. She appeared to support me; however, it was difficult to read. We had some faculty openings in the department; and her support was a little unpredictable. In fact, she rejected the African American very qualified female associate professor who we recommended to be hired. That was a total shock to me that she favored dissenting voices in the department! She did what was humanly possible to become a permanent dean for the school; but, she was fought tooth and nail; as an example, she was not even allowed to apply for the deanship job when the position was opened. Funny enough, she seemed more qualified than the White female dean who was hired; and to appease her, she was promoted to serve as an associate provost for academic affairs. While this sounded like a promotion, in talking to her, she would have liked to serve as the permanent dean of the school of Education. My plight as department chair got worse—the new dean wanted me out of there; and suddenly, the tenure that I was promised by the former interim dean became far-fetched and a mistake that I regretted making in my career. It is critical to note that CCNY is in the heart of Harlem—my

82   *Valuing Other Voices*

presumption was that Africans and African Americans would be all over CCNY; but, that was not the case. I was the highest ranking Black professor in the school and the only Black department chair at CCNY—it was shocking to hear and read about how African Americans had been traditionally mistreated at CCNY.

I left CCNY to become a department head at Valdosta State University. It was a pleasure to come back to the South—there is more honesty about race in the South. The College of Education and Human Services was going through the transformational initiative for Council for the Accreditation of Educator Preparation; and I went to work. Productivity was at high levels programatically and scholarly wise. But, it was a department that had about 10 department head changes in 5 years. The "red flag" was apparent; but, I thought that our higher productivity levels would generate positive changes. But, things went off base when I (a) began to support our new faculty members to avoid losing them; (b) started pushing back on four racist and disruptive senior faculty who thought that they owned the department; (c) gave raises to faculty based on faculty and staff productivity; (d) reduced departmental committees from 16 to 6; (e) changed a long-standing disposition measurement tool from "Concern Form" to "Professional Improvement Plan;" (f) made proactive moves to recruit, retain, and graduate CLD students; (g) demanding changes on the behavioral patterns of the obvious racist and bigoted department secretary. In the end, I felt betrayed by the interim dean who I trusted and who later the interim provost of the university. When he became the interim provost, he appointed a depart adversary to be the interim dean. Even today, I continue to support the junior faculty of that department— they worked very hard and supported my vision and mission as their department head.

INTERVIEWING FOR AND LANDING A DEANSHIP POSITION

It appears that in arts, sciences, engineering, and business, "Africans" have excelled and landed deanship positions, and moved on to be provosts/vice presidents for academic affairs, and even presidents in America's colleges and universities in the United States. In colleges/schools of education, Africans have had difficulty in making it to deanship positions. This is a quagmire that should be vexing to civil rights and social justice advocates—it is a quagmire that has been brewing for a long time and demonstrates a very negative mark on teacher or educator preparation programs in the United States. Sadly, no one seems to care or pay attention! Based on my experiences, interviewing for job to be a dean of a college/school of Education is not an easy undertaking. In other words, it is

Benefits of Educating and Hiring an "African" in America's Higher Education   83

not for the weak-hearted since requirements for a deanship position are not clear—one never knows what to expect. If the position is led by a search firm, one goes through a pre-interview process where a conversation takes place between the applicant and a representative of the search firm. If everything works out well, the person is invited for a telephone, Skype, Zoom, or other forms of interview (e.g., airport interview where the candidate flies to an agreed-upon airport to be interviewed by university representatives). After the interview, a person is invited to a campus visit and interview and this usually takes an average of two days. After on-list and off-list references are checked, and offer is made to the candidate of choice, most probably by the Provost of the college/university. However, some dean searches are done by campus committees—these ones are a little bit more straight-forward, but still has complexities. In all, the wiggle-rooms in interview processes make it easy for discrimination to occur on the bases of race, skin color, gender, sexual orientation, national origin, religion, or personal idiosyncrasy. In efforts to land a Deanship position, I have spoken to more than 50 search firm representatives, done more than 40 interviews via telephone, Skype, Zoom, and other methods, and gone to more than 20 campus visits for interviews.

Though my efforts to land the position of dean seem to have proven fruitless, my experiences have taught me several life lessons. We can all learn a lot from positive and negative experiences. Following are a few of my lessons:

- Your on-list and off-list references matter. Some of your personal references may be your nemesis—they might be highly jealous of you and might not put in the "good words" as expected. One or two on-list references have cost me some opportunities. While off-list references are unpredictable, on-list references should at least be predictable.

- Your national origin, race, skin color, and accent (language) matter. During telephone interviews, accent can have a devastating consequence.

- Being from the African continent can be a struggle—this is connected to national origin, race, culture, and linguistic difference.

- It is not about quality or productivity—it may be about fit and any other reason that the committee or leadership deems okay. The critical question is, "Do they like you?"

- There is no critical mass of Africans and African Americans in leadership positions in colleges and universities. Those that are there may be in survival mode. Not being in where the important decisions are made can be problematic. Very few advocates look like

84   *Valuing Other Voices*

you! Sadly, if a Black person truly likes a Black candidate, he/she has to pretend not to like that candidate to foster serious attention or consideration.

- Black people sometimes do not trust fellow Black people. It is a strange phenomenon—they might want to be the "good nigger" or the only Black person on board. Interestingly, Whites, Indians from Asia, or the Jewish people do not play that retrogressive game.
- Though racism and xenophobia are endemic in higher education, I have received more job and scholarly opportunities from more White people than people of other races, cultures, and languages, including Blacks, Africans, and African Americans.
- Sometimes, it is difficult to know who to trust in higher education— all that glitters may not be gold. To avoid disappointment or heart break, one has to have personal success-oriented plans (i.e., Plans A, B, and even C).

EDUCATIONAL CONSULTANCY IN AMERICA'S SCHOOLS

Educational consultancy involves collaboration and cooperation at different levels (Obiakor, 2001b, 2008, 2018). To be an educational consultant, one must be knowledgeable, current, equipped with cutting-edge ideas, market ideas, willing to share his/her expertise. In addition, one must be a well-known teacher, scholar, researcher, professional, and leader. Consultation does not happen in a vacuum. The question is, If one is not well-respected, how can he/she be invited to be a consultant? Colleges, universities, and school districts invite people who can present and help individuals to shift their paradigms. This process is intertwined with perceptions, assumptions, race, gender, sexual orientation, quality, equity, and personality. It is no surprise that White people are invited to be consultants more than minorities, save for during celebrations such as the Black History Month. This is a major problem at college, university, and school district levels because some people are teaching what they do not know.

Despite traditional and historical impediments, I have been able to serve as a consultant in various arenas. Below are samples of distinguished professor/scholar invitations that afforded me critical opportunities to serve as a consultant:

- Department of Special Education, Palacky University, Olomouc, Czech Republic, October 2015.
- College of Education, Clark Atlanta University, Atlanta, Georgia, March 2010.

- School of Education, the University of North Carolina-Greensboro, Greensboro, North Carolina, February 2010.
- College of Education, Dominican University, River Forest, Illinois, October 2009.
- College of Education, Grambling State University, Grambling, Louisiana, November 2006; April 2008; March 2009.
- McKay College of Education, Brigham Young University, Provo, Utah, March 2001; September 2002; March 2003; March 2005; April 2006; March 2007; December 2008.
- School of Education, Indiana-Purdue University, Fort Wayne, Indiana, February 2007.
- School of Graduate Studies, Center for Continuing and Professional Studies, and School of Education and Urban Studies, Morgan State University, Baltimore, Maryland, April 2005.
- School of Education, Tennessee State University, Nashville, Tennessee, May 2004.
- College of Education Institute for Behavioral and Learning Differences, University of North Texas, Denton, Texas, October – November 2003.
- Center for Educational Practice, St. Xavier University, Chicago, Illinois, March 2003.
- Department of Special Education and Training Culturally Competent Professional (TCCP) Project, Hampton University, Hampton, Virginia, July 2000; July 2001.
- School of Education, Illinois State University, Normal, Illinois, November 2000.
- Institute for the Transformation of Learning, Marquette University, Milwaukee, Wisconsin, October 2000.
- Department of Educational Theory and Practice, Health Sciences Technology Academy, West Virginia University, Morgantown, West Virginia, July 2000.
- Department of Education, Abilene Christian University, Abilene, Texas, April 1999.
- Multicultural Affairs (Student Life), Eastern Illinois University, Charleston, Illinois, February 1998.
- Learning Disability Research and Training Center (LDR&T), The University of Georgia, Athens, Georgia, October 1995.
- Department of Special Education, College of Education, Portland State University, Portland, Oregon, Summer 1995.

86 *Valuing Other Voices*

- Black Cultural Center, Indiana University of Pennsylvania, Indiana, Pennsylvania, February 1994.
- Department of English, African Literature, Hendrix College, Conway, Arkansas, Summer 1993.
- Student Support Services/Disabled Student Services Program, Frostburg State University, Frostburg, Maryland, February 1988.

CONCLUSION

This chapter unveils my personal experiences as an "African" in America's colleges and universities. These experiences may be different from those of other Africans in higher education; however, in talking to others, our experiences seem to be similar. We came from strange lands to succeed in a strange land; and that is a good thing. While coming to America has been a fruitful journey, we have endured so much to survive and be successful. Personally, I have learned a lot; and I am convinced that many people have learned a lot from me. I have always known that I am a hard worker dedicated to excellence; however, I never knew that I will be a successful and well-known teacher, scholar, professional, and leader. These mean that the idea of being a "shithole" person who comes from a "shithole" country or continent to the United States does not make sense or hold water.

The fact remains that what we do in higher education should be very measurable; and measurably, I have produced and continue to produce at all levels. And, other Africans have continued to produce in America's colleges and universities despite the predicaments that they confront on daily basis. In teaching, they bring in new voices and new perspectives. In research and scholarship, they write grants and publish consistently; and in their professions, they continue to make a difference. The question then is, How are Africans rewarded for their hard works? In colleges/schools of education, they hang on shoe strings; and their names are not seen or heard in scholarly and leadership circles. As a commitment, I have been working hard to shatter the glass ceiling; but, it has been difficult. Hopefully, with time, traditional walls will be knocked down.

Finally, through this chapter, I am happy to have succeeded in debunking the myth that Africa and Africans are "shithole" people who are irrelevant to the well-being and progress of the United States. For me, coming to America and getting involved with America's higher education have been rewarding (e.g., I met my wife at New Mexico State University; and as I indicated, we have been blessed). In addition, some of my former students and mentees have excelled in their chosen areas of interest; and more importantly, I have continued to mentor new teachers, researchers, scholars, professionals, and leaders. In the end, it is my hope that newcomers to higher education will learn the trials and tribulations of the professorial game.

CHAPTER 11

"BANGWAGON EFFECT" ON THINKING AND SOCIETY TOWARD MULTICULTURAL PROBLEM SOLVING

Is thinking dead? Why do we continue to have the lingering issues that we have in our society and world? How do we think our way into a progressive pattern of living instead of living our way into a retrogressive system of thinking? How do we avoid the "bandwagon effect" on our thinking and society? And, how do we address our vexing problems in our respective communities, regions, states, nations, and world without thinking and asking questions? These are central questions that we must continue to ask and answer if we are to solve the endemic problems confronting the globe. Growing up in Nigeria, I have experienced British colonialism, national independence, tribalism, political conflicts, military coups, religious killings, pogrom, the perils of the Nigeria/Biafra war, and tyrannical/unpatriotic leadership (Soyinka, 1994). When the war ended in 1970, my whole family members were happy and excited. No more hunger! No more kwashiorkor! No more diseases! No more disruptions! No more disasters! No more blockade! And, no more darkness! We saw a gloomy light at the end of the tunnel! Even though there was some light, there were some somber realities. Many people had died! Many souls were lost! And, sometimes, the reason for the war was lost! Rather than renew and reinvigorate the quest for unity, equanimity, and progress in Nigeria, the

Valuing Other Voices: Discourses That Matter in Education, Social Justice, and Multiculturalism, pp. 89–96

Copyright © 2020 by Information Age Publishing

All rights of reproduction in any form reserved.

90 *Valuing Other Voices*

selfish Nigerian leaders did not think and learn—they were short-sighted and interested in the self-aggrandizement of winning the war; and as a result, we were back to square one. During that period, we were excited about the end of the war not because we hated the war that prevented an extensive pogrom against the Ibos (my Biafra people), but because we were sick and tired of being sick and tired. The world had forgotten and betrayed us! In my defeated youthful mind, the world had allowed the Hausa/Fulani oligarchy (mostly Muslims) to destroy, dominate, and diminish the Ibos/the people of Biafra (mostly Christians). Based on my tribal pride, this was unconscionable! As an Ibo, I felt broken; but, with time, I have learned and grown to remain strong. I have found solace in R. H. Sin's works, especially in the poem, "Create More," in the 2017 book, *A Beautiful Composition of Broken*. As the poem reads,

> Don't let your past corrupt
> the present
> don't let the painful memories
> you've created
> keep you from the creation
> of something better. (p. 230)

Today, the disappointment of the Nigeria/Biafra war is something that many Ibos have not forgotten, even when they pretend or try to. Looking at Nigeria some decades later, the domination and disappointment of the Ibos have continued to exist and even flourish. Many critical thinkers see these situations as explosions that continue to be swept under the rug in Nigeria! Hopefully, some right-thinking Nigerian and world leaders will work very hard to "think deeper" about solutions that finally could bring the Ibos and many other tribes into the Nigerian fold. In my thinking, I believe the Ibos themselves can never come out of this quagmire, unless they themselves put on their thinking hats to reassess their sacred existence as powerful entities capable of (a) thinking creatively to redeem their very lost souls, (b) enhancing the quality and quantity of their value and stock, and (c) thinking their way into a new pattern of living that fosters innovative endeavors at all critical levels. Clearly, the Ibos have been unable to live their way into a retrogressive and denigrating system of thinking that is pervasively perpetuated in Nigeria, an excellent example of a country that is immorally, corruptly, and unpatriotically led in the world.

Though I was happy that the war had ended like many Ibos, as a youth, I was not impressed with our adults and leaders thought in Nigeria! I could not believe the world would be so unkind and so silent to condone such wicked and destructive actions against a group of human beings. I could not help but ask my father, a man with a second grade education, why the war went the way it did. After my question, my father laughed as he usually did and responded: "Son, human beings are smart; but, many think with one-quarter of their brains" (Chief Charles O. Obiakor, Sr., 1970). While this powerful statement remains with me today, I do not know how my father arrived at this conclusion because he was neither a researcher nor a scientist. As a young inquisitive mind, I began to think about the rationale for my father's statement to see if I could garner the scientific support for his assertion. That got me interested in (a) reading a lot, (b) becoming a teacher, (c) thinking about how the brain works, and (d) exploring new knowledge such as special education. As I began to study special education in the graduate school, I began to wonder if human beings truly maximize their potential to think. I have found that in my own life, most human beings hate to think, especially when it comes to challenging systemic underpinnings and arrogant proclamations. I began to discover that intelligences are multidimensional; that people think in different ways; that systems can impinge upon how people think; and that with the band wagon effect on communication today, the society is faced with picking up information that may be true or false. While this sounds abnormal, we cannot discount the impact of any news, in these days of technology. After all, our goal is to have the ability to differentiate between what is real news, fake news, or "alternative facts" (Conway, 2017).

Based on the aforementioned, I can now see why my father conceptualized his own common sense theory of people thinking with one-quarter of their brains (i.e., about 25% of their brains). In my interactions with people, I have heard other people remark that "people only think with 10% of their brains," less than my father's percentage. I am unclear as to the foundational roots of these remarks and presumptions; however, one can rightfully state that there are at least some discussions about the thinking of the mind and brain at some quarters (Della Sala, 1999). For example, Beyerstein (1987, 1999) tried in his works to discount "the myth that we only use ten percent of our brains" to think and live. While I am not a brain researcher or surgeon, I do know that all people do not think alike; and that some people are more forward-looking in their thinking than others.

WHY ALL THE FUSS ABOUT THINKING AND SOCIETAL ADVANCEMENT?

Thinking is a powerful tool when used appropriately. When thinking is unused, the society suffers. On the other hand, when education is interwoven with thinking, people grow, experience, experiment, do, act, discover, create, and invent (Beachum & Obiakor, 2018; Gibson & Obiakor, 2018; Obiakor, 2018). For example, in great democratic nations such as

92 *Valuing Other Voices*

Canada, France, Germany, and the United States, leaders are democratically elected and education is framed to reflect the ability to grow via the freedom to think or "question and answer." In communist, socialist, and dictatorial governments such as Russia, China, and North Korea, leaders serve for longer terms and frequently enjoy imposed power that is forced on the people and education fails to encourage the "question and answer" method. Is it any surprise that in democracies, citizens think their ways into a pattern of living; and in communist, socialist, and dictatorial governments, people live their ways into a system of thinking?

As indicated, thinking people learn, experiment, experience, explore, and discover. These behaviors are embedded in good educational environments where the human mind is allowed to grow and expand to renew itself. Educational renewal leads to societal renewal, and vice versa. In his work on what true education entails, John Dewey (1897) argued that:

> Education proceeds by the participation of the individual in the social consciousness of the race. This process begins unconsciously almost at birth, and is continually shaping the individual's powers, saturating his [her] habits, training his [her] ideas, and arousing his [her] feelings and emotions. Through this unconscious education the individual gradually comes to share in the intellectual and moral resources which humanity has succeeded in getting together. (p.1)

Based on Dewey's (1897) statement above, education can never be divorced from human thinking and action. In other words, actionable thinking involves education and problem-solving, and vice versa. This idea of actionable thinking was expanded by Dr. Benjamin Bloom (1956) in his book, *Taxonomy of Educational Objectives: The Classification of Educational Goals* when he discussed and described how three domains of learning (i.e., *cognitive, affective, and psychomotor*) interact with hierarchical thinking processes of *knowledge, comprehensive, application, analysis, synthesis, and evaluation*. For example, problem-solving, when effectively done, creates a "question and answer" environment where people see themselves as a part of the learning process and solution. In the same vein, most problem-solvers attempt to (a) identify the issues, (b) understand everyone's interests, (c) list possible solutions, (d) evaluate options, (e) select an option or options, (f) document agreement or agreements, and (h) agree on contingencies, monitoring, and evaluation (Hicks, 2018). How can we judge assumptions underlying personal and group ideas and efforts if critical thinking and problem-solving are not fully considered or if they are allowed to die? How can communities, nations, and our world move forward to advance society's needs if our thinking is static or retrogressive? It is no surprise that authoritarian and autocratic leaderships do not favor critical problem-solving that advances thinking. We

"Bangwagon Efffect" on Thinking and Society 93

know that historically such leaderships have forced their people to follow and not challenge ideas, policies, rules, and regulations. When thinking is devalued, problem-solving is dishonored, societies are not uplifted, and peoples suffer.

BEING CAREFUL ABOUT THE
"BANDWAGON EFFECT" ON THINKING

As an undergraduate student in Nigeria, I studied the "bandwagon effect on demand" in one of my economic classes. It was a fascinating topic to me! In my further reading on the topic, I found that "bandwagon effect" transcends economics, fashion, politics, individual popularity, society, and so on. In all situations, the explanations of "bandwagon effect" are not that different. As I understand it, "bandwagon effect" is a psychological phenomenon whereby actions and beliefs of individuals are emulated by others based on the information that they derive from them. Based on this broad conceptualization, the popularity of a product or phenomenon can encourage more people to like it; and the hatred of a product or phenomenon can motivate more people to hate it. Considering some recent fashion trends, hip-hop music, dancing styles, politics, customs, fads, and beliefs, to mention a few, one can conclude that "bandwagon effect" can increase sociocultural valuation or sociocultural devaluation. Many authors (e.g., Asch, 1955; Coleman, 2003; Nadeau, Cloutier, & Guay, 1993) have attempted to write on bandwagon effects in different life-engaging situations. For instance, Asch (1955) focused on opinions and social pressure; Nadeau et al. (1993) presented new evidence about the existence of a bandwagon effect in the opinion formation process; and Coleman (2003) explained the bandwagon phenomenon in the *Oxford Dictionary of Psychology*. These efforts continue to attract researchers, scholars, and educators.

In the 2016 presidential elections in the United States, there were waves of facts, unsubstantiated facts, or alternative facts that people believed because they became popular. While it is still unclear as to their influence in the election of President Donald J. Trump, one cannot totally discount their influence in people's thinking and action at some micro and macro levels. Such influence can be explained as a "bandwagon effect" or what some people call the "herd mentality." In the former Soviet Union and in today's Russia, people live their ways into a system of thinking rather than think their ways into a pattern of living. For example, in Russia, President Putin was elected with large numbers. People who oppose him are frequently viewed as traitors and die in mysterious ways. Those who question him are caricatured, ridiculed, and eliminated.

94   Valuing Other Voices

In contrast, we have had many presidents elected in the United States since President Putin came to power in Russia. When the citizens are forced to think alike and not ask questions, no thinking takes place and decisions are not functionally goal-directed. Apparently, to be safe in places like Russia and governments that lack freedom, people join the bandwagon and tolerate their own devalued existence.

Thinking is a supreme gift to a free people; yet, it is frequently taken for granted. The critical question is, How can socioeconomic, political, educational, and cultural advancements be achieved in environments that do not encourage thinking and questioning? In ancient Greece, Socrates questioned the authenticity of the Sophists in framing the well-being of the Athenian youth; and before long, he was accused and killed for corrupting the youth. Interestingly, the Socratic method of instruction gained its origin through this historical phenomenon. Below are the aftereffects of the lack of thinking in our society:

- *Slave mentality*—This manifests itself as mental enslavement.
- *Herd mentality*—This occurs when the masses follow orders like animals.
- *Political upheaval*—This occurs when there is serious political unrest.
- *Social unrest*—This occurs with the society revolts and there is anarchy.
- *Tribalism*—This occurs when favors are done for tribesmen and woman despite capability or incapability.
- *Military coup*—This occurs when the military takes over a government.
- *Barbaric killing*—This occurs when people join a band of agitators and killers to kill others.
- *Pogrom*—This occurs when the masses are convinced to join others to kill a group of people with the intention of eliminating them form the face of the earth.
- *Religious animus*—This occurs when people of one religion detest people of another religion.
- *Dictatorship*—This occurs when people take advantage of their dictate powers to victimize the masses.
- *Racism*—This occurs as a result of racial animus (i.e., hatred of a person of another race).
- *Paternalism*—This occurs when people treat people like their children.
- *Messiah complex*—This occurs when people play God and savior while ignoring the strengths of others.

- *Fraudulent multiculturalism*—This occurs when people pretend to be more multicultural than they really are.
- *Xenophobia*—This occurs when people show tremendous animus against foreigners.
- *Homophobia*—This occurs when people detest people because of their sexual orientation.
- *Terrorism*—This occurs when innocent citizens are hurt and killed by well-planned hateful and deadly actions.
- *Phony loyalty*—This occurs when there appears to be loyalty that does not exist.

CONCLUSION

Thinking is a critical element of the human endeavor; and the goal of any human being must be to think his/her way into a pattern of living instead of living his/her way into a system of thinking. While some cultures are individualistic; others are community-based. This does not mean that the individual's brain should be sacrificed for group thinking. Ignoring the individual's mind is like sending him/her to jail where orders and punishments are hourly or daily calls. In such situations, the human potential is never maximized.

Today, the world needs critical thinking leaders at micro and macro levels. Emotions alone cannot help or save us. In fact, in many cases, our emotions have hurt us—they have led to assumptions, generalizations, and inhumane actions. Our educational systems must be designed to focus on critical thinking, divergent thinking, and problem solving. We need to revisit our thinking about important socioeducational constructs in our institutions. For example, we know and recognize that our intelligences and self-concepts are multidimensional; yet, we continue to globalize these constructs. Why are we consistently toying around with the future of our children and youth? Why do we continue to misidentify, mismeasure, mislabel, misplace, and miseducate fellow humans even when our thinking tells us that they are wrong? Why do we continue to struggle with change even when we know that it is the only way for us to improve ourselves?

Finally, experience matters and leadership matters! We do not have to reinvent the wheels. It is time we started "thinking deeper" about improving the educational outcomes of vulnerable children and the citizens of our world. When we take thinking seriously, we will resolve some of our most difficult problems and make the world a better place in which to live. It is not enough to join the bandwagon in the name of patriotism,

96 *Valuing Other Voices*

supremacy, love of race, religious affiliation, culture, or value, to mention a few. Let us join the bandwagon to improve the educational outcomes of vulnerable children! Let us join the bandwagon to do something good so that we can thoroughly maximize our potentials as human beings! Let us "create more" by not allowing our painful past to blind our thinking! And, in the end, let us "think more" to relieve our sacred but burdened souls.

AFTERWORD

Listening to Other Voices and Continuing Our Discourses

Carol Huang
Department of Leadership and Special Education
The City College of New York, City University of New York

It is a privilege to write this afterword for Dr. Festus E. Obiakor's book, *Valuing Other Voices: Discourses That Matter in Education, Social, and Multiculturalism*. Dr. Obiakor is a former colleague and department chair at the City College of New York, The City University of New York. In this book, as an African immigrant scholar, he expresses his views on multiculturalism, Blackness, social justice, and other related issues. As an Asian American immigrant woman, educated by a revered African American scholar, James D. Anderson, I learned a lot from his classes and stories. I still remember one of his stories vividly. While traveling by bus with an African classmate to the South during one of his semester breaks, he was shocked by his classmate's behavior. As a person who grew up in the South, Dr. Anderson knew the code of conduct to keep himself safe in the pre-Brown era. He would avoid leaving the bus at stops unless it was absolutely necessary. But, his classmate had no such inhibitions. He went off the bus as much as he wanted to look around and speak with Whites there. At one point, when he returned to the bus, he even touched one of the White passengers walking through the isle to his seat. Dr. Anderson was worried

---

Valuing Other Voices: Discourses That Matter in Education, Social Justice,
and Multiculturalism, pp. 97–100
Copyright © 2020 by Information Age Publishing
All rights of reproduction in any form reserved.

97

98 *Valuing Other Voices*

for their safety; but, they arrived without being harmed. Dr. Anderson commented: "They (the Whites) knew he was from Africa so they did not do anything to him." Clearly, my message here is that those who discriminate against others are ignorant; but, they can be also very intentional in their negative actions. Throughout this book, Obiakor highlights and exposes this important message.

In this book, Obiakor reiterates that our awareness of our assumed social position informs our behavior in our environment. Oppression has memory and steers our paths and informs our behavior. Frequently, African scholars searching for their voices take rather different paths from African Americans because the world they grew up in is different. When they enter the United States as immigrants from Africa, they experience the same policies that stratified African American communities from the foundational pillars of the United States. As a result, their struggle to gain justice and find a niche in the United States follows the same continuum of oppression; and thus, their scholarship supports the marginalized, disabled, disfranchised, and oppressed. Obiakor's message, in this book, is clear: Let us value all human-beings and treat them with equanimity.

PRACTICING EQUITY: IMPACT ON WHAT WE DO

Walking in the hallways of the School of Education at the University of Illinois at Urbana-Champaign with the very diverse student population in my Ph D cohort and also from the only African American chair in the School of Education, I learned to be multicultural. As the department chair, Dr. Anderson dutifully stationed himself in his office facing the hallway so that each student passing through his office door could greet him and be greeted in return. Throughout the day, the greeting would switch from "Dr. Anderson" to "Dr." to "Hi" to "Hey" to making eye contacts with a hand gesture or wink. But, we all knew we had to greet him when we passed through his office. So many years after graduating, the greeting through the day when I worked in the teaching assistant office remains a memorable ritual of my PhD years. The greeting actually was a practice of equality, equity, and willingness to acknowledge as many people in the department as he could as a chair. And, I am still affected by the feeling and the attention he gave me when I walked by his door. When he got the mentorship grant from American Education Research Association, we all were granted travel grants to attend the association's annual conferences to present our papers. When we flew out from the tiny airport of Champaign, we were all excited and arrived early for the flight. But, he was late and the flight attendant barred him from boarding. I thought they did that because he is African American; and I got extremely upset and went to tell the attendant that I would not board if the one who paid for us to take the flight could not board the flight. Eventually, he was on the same flight like every graduate student of his. It became clear to us that discrimination is rampant! But, he took it with grace and did not let it bother him at least from what I had observed. I knew I would blow up if I were in his situation. Obiakor, in *Valuing Other Voices: Discourses That Matter in Education, Social Justice, and Multiculturalism* shares many stories and incidents of similar nature and describes how to survive in the face of adversities.

As we celebrated the 50th anniversary of *Brown v Board of Education*, Orfield, Ee, Frankenberg, and Siegel-Hawley (2016) at the Harvard Civil Rights Project, painted a gloomy result of our nation's desegregation history. We were shocked to realize that Brown might not have delivered what we wished it to accomplish (Anderson, 2004, 2006). For example, Fessenden (2012) explained that New York City had about 1,600 public schools and over 800 of them had more than 90% minorities in them. According to Orfield et al. (2016), New York City schools is the most segregated in the United States with only 15.7% Black (ranked worst in the nation) and 20.4% Latino students (ranked third in the nation next to California and Texas). As a professor at The City College of New York, I have found that many of my students did not go to public schools with other races; and I might be the only Asian, Taiwanese-American teacher they ever had. These examples have proven that racism is alive and well! This is the major point that Obiakor, in this book, makes time and time again.

Through the years, I have switched my focus from aiming directly at the erosion of the dreams and hopes raised by *Brown* to focus on the story of Charles Hamilton Houston, the dean of Howard Law School, who used the school as an incubator to grow a generation of civil rights lawyers and built the momentum that led to the *Brown* decision. In *Valuing Other Voices: Discourses That Matter in Education, Social Justice, and Multiculturalism*, Obiakor emphasizes the importance of a generational vision of teachers and students to build the foundations for social justice and human valuing. It is my wish for my students as a teaching force in the extremely segregated New York City to know this vision. In my fieldworks, I have observed how multiculturalism is taught in the classroom and witnessed that it is dwindling and almost non-existent. While we live in a city with a diverse population, we go on our separate ways consistent with our school system. As Obiakor noted, in this book, we must "value other voices" and improve our discourses to bring back the Brown's vision and figure ways to get out of our current darkness of disenfranchisement.

CONCLUSION

Valuing Other Voices: Discourses That Matter in Education, Social Justice, and Multiculturalism is a book that can serve as a resource in changing our current discriminatory practices at this critical juncture. The emerging voices of foreign born scholars like Obiakor are demanding to be valued and heard. Even though the numbers of African born scholars in the United States are small, their voices need to be taken seriously. When I first started teaching in New York City in 2005, the foreign-born population in the United States was 36 million; and it is projected to rise to 81 million by 2050 when the minority population in the United States will reach 56% and current minorities will become the majority (Pew Research Center, 2008).

Finally, in this book, Obiakor urges all of us to hear other voices, but concludes that this will only happen when many disenfranchised people value their own voices and push to be heard. We must continue our discourses on issues related to vulnerable and disillusioned populations. Colleges/schools of educations must infuse multiculturalism in their systemic reformation of courses and curricula; and all stakeholders and accreditation agencies must make sure that our current and future teachers are well-prepared to deal with demographic changes in schools and society. It is important that we add this book to our reading list—graduate students, general and special education professionals, community leaders and stakeholders, and government agencies must engage in fearless conversations and programmatic re-orientations to help every learner to maximize his/her potential. In the end, by reading this book, we will be listening to other voices and continuing our discourses.

REFERENCES

Anderson, J. D. (2004, July). Crosses to bear and promises to keep: The jubilee anniversary of *Brown v. Board of Education*. *Urban Education, 39*(4), 359–373.

Anderson, J. D. (2006, October). A tale of two '*Browns*': Constitutional equality and unequal education. *Yearbook of the National Society for the Study of Education, 105*(2), 14–35

Fessenden, F. (2012, May 11). A portrait of segregation in New York City's schools. Retrieved from https://archive.nytimes.com/www.nytimes.com/interactive/2012/05/11/nyregion/segregation-in-new-york-city-public-schools.html

Orfield, G., Ee, J., Frankenberg, E., & Siegel-Hawley, G. (2016). *Brown* at 62: School segregation by race, poverty and state, Civil Rights Project. Retrieved from https://escholarship.org/uc/item/5ds6k0rd

Pew Research Center. (2008). *U.S. Population Projections: 2005-2050*. Washington, DC: Author.

REFERENCES

Anderson, J. D. (2004). Crosses to bear and promises to keep: The Jubilee Anniversary of *Brown v. Board of Education*. *Urban Education, 39*(4), 359–373.

Anderson, J. D. (2006). A tale of two 'Browns': Constitutional equality and inequal education. *Yearbook of the National Society for the Study of Educating, 105*(2), 14–35.

Amman, M. (2002). Foreword: Blacks, Whites, and a cultural divide: Revelations of my American journey. In F. E. Obiakor & P. A. Grant (Eds.), *Foreign- born African Americans: Silenced voices in the discourse on race* (pp. xi- xvii). New York, NY: Nova Science.

Amman, M. (2003). And don't call me arrogant. In F. E. Obiakor & J. U. Gordon (Eds.), *African perspectives in American higher education* (pp. 105–115). New York, NY: Nova Science.

Asch, S. E. (1955). Opinions and social pressure. *Scientific American, 193*(5), 31–35.

Beachum, F. D., & Obiakor, F. E. (2018). *Improving outcomes of vulnerable children.* San Diego, CA: Plural.

Bell, D. (1985). *And we are not saved: The elusive quest for racial justice.* New York, NY: Basic Books.

Bell, D. (1992). *Faces at the bottom of the wall: The permanence of racism.* New York, NY: Basic Books.

Bennis W. (1989). *On becoming a leader.* Reading, MA: Addison-Wesley.

Beyerstein, B. L. (1987). The brain and consciousness: Implications for the psi phenomena. *The Skeptical Inquiry, 12*(2), 163–173.

Beyenstein, B. L. (1999). When cometh the myth that we only use ten percent of our brains? In S. Della Sala (Ed.), *Mind myths: Exploring everyday mysteries of the mind and brain* (pp. 1–24). Chichester, England: John Wiley and Sons.

Binet, A. (1909). *Les ideas modernes sur les enfants* [Modern ideas for children]. Paris, France: Hammarion.

Blackhurst, A. E., & Berdine, W. H. (1993). *An introduction to special education* (3rd ed.). New York, NY: Harper Collins.

Valuing Other Voices: Discourses That Matter in Education, Social Justice, and Multiculturalism, pp. 101–108
Copyright © 2020 by Information Age Publishing
All rights of reproduction in any form reserved.

102   Valuing Other Voices

Bloom, B. (1956). *Taxonomy of educational objectives: The classification of educational goals*. New York, NY: David McKay.

Bolsta, P. (2008, May). Executive interview: Tim Solso. *WorldTraveler*, p. 64.

Brown v. Board of Education of Topeka Kansas, 347 U.S. 483, 745-ct-686, 98 L.Ed. 873, 530. 0. 326 (1954).

Canfield, J., & Siconne, F. (1993). *101 ways to develop student self-esteem* (Vol. 1). Boston, MA: Allyn & Bacon.

Canfield, J., & Wells, H. C. (1976). *100 ways to enhance self-concept in the classroom*. Englewood Cliffs, NJ: Prentice Hall.

Chetty, R., Henderson, N., Jones, M. R., & Porter, S. R. (2018). *The Equality of Opportunity Project*. Retrieved from www.equalityofopportunity.org

Chow, K. (2017, April 8). *"Model minority" myth again used as a racial wedge between Asians and Blacks*. Code Switch Podcast, National Public Radio (NPR), Washington, DC.

Civil Rights Act (1964), Pub, L. No. 88-352.

Collins, H. T., & Zakariya, S. B. (1982). *Getting started in global education: A primer for principals and teachers*. Arlington, VA: National Association of Elementary School Principals.

Coleman, A. (2003). *Oxford dictionary of psychology*. New York, NY: Oxford University Press.

Conway, K. (2017, January 22). *Alternative facts*. Interview on "Meet The Press" hosted by Chuck Todd, Washington, DC.

Council for the Accreditation of Educator Preparation (2013). *Origin of CAEP*. Washington, DC: Author.

Cullinan, D., & Kauffman, J. M. (2005, August). Do race of student and race of teacher influence ratings of emotional and behavioral problem characteristics of students with emotional disturbance? *Behavioral Disorders, 30*, 393–402.

Della Sala, S. (1999). *Mind myths: Exploring everyday mysteries of the mind and brain*. England, United Kingdom: John Wiley and Sons.

Dewey, J. (1897). *My pedagogical creed*. New York, NY: E. L. Kellogg & Co.

Dewey, J. (1958). *Philosophy of education*. Ames, IA: Littlefield, Adams & Co.

D'Souza, D. (1996). *The end of racism: Principles for a multiracial society*. Washington, DC: Free Press.

D'Souza, D. (1998). *Illiberal education: The politics of race and sex on campus*. Washington, DC: Free Press.

Education of All Handicapped Children Act (1975), Pub. L. No. 94-142.

Education of All Handicapped Children Act Amendments (1986), Pub. L. No 99-457.

Ellison, R. (1952). *The invisible man*. London, England: Random House.

Every Child Succeeds Act (2015). Pub. L. 114-95.

Feagin, J., & Chou, R. (2008). *The myth of the model minority Asian Americans facing racism*. Boulder, CO: Paradigm.

Fessenden, F. (2012, May 11). A portrait of segregation in New York City's schools. Retrieved from https://archive.nytimes.com/www.nytimes.com/interactive/2012/05/11/nyregion/segregation-in-new-york-city-public-schools.html

Ford, B. A., Obiakor, F. E., & Patton, J. M. (1995). *Effective education for African American exceptional learners: New perspectives*. Austin, TX: Pro-Ed.

References   103

Friedman, T. L., & Mandelbaum, M. (2012). *That used to be us: How America fell behind in the world it invented and how we can come back.* New York, NY: Picador.

Gardner, H. (1993). *Multiple intelligences: The theory of practice.* New York, NY: Basic Books.

Gibson, L., & Obiakor, F. E. (2018). *Computer-based technology for special and multicultural education: Enhancing 21st century learning.* San Diego, CA: Plural.

Goldstein, A. P. (1999). *The prepare curriculum: Teaching prosocial competencies.* Champaign, IL: Research Press.

Goleman, D. (1995). *Emotional intelligence: Why it matters more than IQ.* New York, NY: Bantam Books.

Goodlad, J. I. (1983). Access to knowledge. In J. I. Goodlad & T. L. Lovitt (Eds.), *Integrating general and special education* (pp. 1–22). New York, NY: Merrill.

Gould, S. J. (1981). *The mismeasure of man.* New York, NY: W. W. Morton.

Haberman, M. (1995). *Star teachers of children in poverty.* West Lafayette, IN: Kappa Delta Pi.

Harris, M. (2011). *Self-responsibility of African American parents in the education of their secondary students with disabilities.* Unpublished PhD dissertation, Urban Education and Exceptional Education, University of Wisconsin-Milwaukee, Milwaukee, WI.

Helper, M. M. (1955). Learning theory and self-concept. *Journal of Abnormal and Social Psychology, 5*, 184–194.

Hicks, T. (2018). Seven steps for effective problem solving in the workplace. Retrieved from *Mediate.com*

Hilliard, A. G. (1992, October/November). The pitfalls and practices of special education practice. *Exceptional Children, 59*, 168–172.

Holmes, B. C. (1994). *Like a lasting storm: Helping with real life problems.* Brandon, VT: Clinical Psychology.

Individuals with Disabilities Education Act (1990), Pub. L. No. 101-476.

Individuals with Disabilities Education Act (1997), Pub L. No. 105-17.

Individuals with Disabilities Education Improvement Act (2004), Pub. L. No. 108-446.

James, W. (1958). *Talk to teachers on psychology, and to students on life's ideas.* New York, NY: W. W. Norton.

Katsiyannis, A., Yell, M. L., & Bradley, R. (2001). Reflections of the 25th anniversary of the individuals with exceptionalities education act. *Remedial and Special Education,22*(6), 324–339.

Kauffman, J. M. (2002). *Education deform? Bright people sometimes say stupid things about education.* Lanham, MD: Scarecrow Education.

Kauffman, J. M. (2003a, May). Reflections on the field. *Behavioral Disorders, 28*, 205–208.

Kauffman, J. M. (2003b, July/August). Appearances, stigma, and prevention. *Remedial and Special Education, 24*, 195–198.

Kauffman, J. M. (2004). The president's commission and the devaluation of special education. *Education and Treatment of Children, 27*, 307–324.

Keogh, B. K. (1990, October/November). Narrowing the gap between policy and practice. *Exceptional Children, 57*(2), 186–190.

104 Valuing Other Voices

King, C. S. (1983). *The words of Martin Luther King, Jr.* New York, NY: Newmarket Press.

King, M. L., Jr. (1957, November). *Loving your enemies.* Presentation at Dexter Avenue Baptist Church, Montgomery, AL.

King, M. L., Jr. (1967, April). *Beyond Vietnam: A time to break silence.* Presentation at Riverside Church, New York.

Kouzes, J. M., & Posner, B. Z. (2007). *The leadership challenge* (4th ed.). San Francisco, CA: Jossey-Bass.

Li, G., & Wang, L. (2008). *Model minority myth revisited: An interdisciplinary* approach to demystifying Asian American educational experiences. Charlotte, NC: Information Age.

Lieberman, L. M. (2001, January 17). The death of special education. *Education Week*, pp. 39–41.

Long, N. J. (1997). The therapeutic power of kindness. *Reclaiming Children and Youth, 5*, 242–246.

Marsh, H. W., Parker, J., & Barnes, J. (1985). Multidimensional adolescent self-concepts: Their relationships to age, sex, and academic measures. *American Educational Research Journal, 22*(3), 422–444.

Marsh, H. W., & Smith, I. D. (1986). Cross national study of the structure and level of multidimensional self-concepts: An application of confirmatory factor analysis. *Resources in Education, 21*(9), 192. (ERIC Reproduction Service No. ED 269 429).

Marshall, H. H. (1989, July). The development of self-concept. *Young Children, 44*(5), 44–51.

McFarland, L. J., Senn, L. E., & Childress, J. R. (1993). *21st century leadership: Dialogues with 100 top leaders.* New York, NY: The Leadership Press.

Mechanic, D., & Tanner, J. (2015). Vulnerable people, groups, and populations: Societal view. *Health Affairs, 26*(5), 1220–1230.

Mills v. Board of Education of the District of Columbia (1992). 348 f. Supp. 866 (D.D.C.1972)

Minton, H., & Schneider, F. (1985). *Differential psychology.* Prospect Heights, IL: Waveland Press.

Mostert, M. P., Kauffman, J. M., & Kavale, K. A. (2003, August). Truth and consequences. *Behavioral Disorders, 28*, 333–347.

Mukuria, G., & Obiakor, F. E. (2004). Special education issues and African diaspora. *Journal of International Special Needs Education, 7*, 12–17.

Muller, D. (1978). Self-concept: A new alternative for education. *College of Education Dialogue Series Monograph.* Las Cruces, NM: New Mexico State University. (ERIC Reproduction Service No. ED 165 067).

Muller, D., Chambliss, J., & Muller, A. (1982, October). *Enhancing self-concept in the classroom.* Paper presented at the annual conference of the National Education Association of New Mexico, Las Cruces, NM.

Nadeau, R., Cloutier, E., & Guay, J. H. (1993). New evidence about the existence of a bandwagon effect in the opinion formation process. *International Political Science Review, 14*(2), 203–213.

No Child Left Behind Act (2001), Pub. L. No. 107–110.

References   105

Obiakor, F. E. (1990, November). *Self-concept of young children: What teachers and parents should know.* Paper presented at the 36th annual Tennessee Association of Young Children Conference, Chattanooga, TN.

Obiakor, F. E. (1992a). Self-image and fatherhood. *Vision Chattanooga: A Publication of the Chattanooga Resource Foundation, 2*(1), 7.

Obiakor, F. E. (1992b). Self-concept of African American students: An operational model for special education. *Exceptional Children, 59*(2), 160–167.

Obiakor, F. E. (1999). Teacher expectations of minority exceptional learners: Impact on "accuracy" of self-concepts. *Exceptional Children, 66,* 39–53.

Obiakor, F. E. (2001a). Developing emotional intelligence in learners with behavioral problems: Refocusing special education. *Behavior Disorders, 26,* 321–331.

Obiakor, F. E. (2001b). *It even happens in good schools: Responding to cultural diversity in today's classrooms.* Thousand Oaks, CA: Corwin Press.

Obiakor, F. E. (2002). Foreign-born Black males: The invisible voices. In J. U. Gordon (Ed.), *The Black male in White America* (pp. 183–193). Hauppauge, NY: Nova Science.

Obiakor, F. E. (2003). *To assess or not, is that the question? Who benefits from the No Child Left Behind Act?* Invited scholar presentation sponsored by the Institute on Multicultural Relations and the Milwaukee Urban League, University of Wisconsin-Milwaukee, Milwaukee, WI.

Obiakor, F. E. (2004). Impact of changing demographics on public education for culturally diverse learners with behavior problems: Implications for teacher preparation. In L. M. Bullock & R. A. Gable (Eds.), *Quality personnel preparation in emotional/behavioral disorders: Current perspectives and future directions* (pp. 51–63). Denton, TX: Institute for Behavioral and Learning Differences at the University of North Texas.

Obiakor, F. E. (2007). *Multicultural special education: Culturally responsive teaching.* Upper Saddle River, NJ: Pearson/Merrill Prentice Hall.

Obiakor, F. E. (2008). *The eight-step approach to multicultural learning and teaching* (3rd ed.). Dubuque, IA: Kendall/Hunt.

Obiakor, F. E. (2009). Educating African American urban learners: Brown in context. In M. C. Brown II & R. D. Bartee (Eds.), *The broken cisterns of African American education* (pp. 61–72). Charlotte, NC: Information Age.

Obiakor, F. E. (2017). *The town crier calls.* Milwaukee, WI: Cissus.

Obiakor, F. E. (2018). *Powerful multicultural essays for innovative educators and leaders: Optimizing "hearty" conversations.* Charlotte, NC: Information Age.

Obiakor, F. E., & Algozzine, B. (Eds.). (1995a). Educating learners with problem behaviors: An unresolved issue for general and special educators. In *Managing problem behaviors: Perspectives for general and special educators* (pp. 1–19). Dubuque, IA: Kendall/Hunt.

Obiakor, F. E., & Algozzine, B. (1995b, December). Self-concept of young children with special needs: Perspectives for school and clinic. *Canadian Journal of School Psychology, 10*(2), 123–130.

Obiakor, F. E., & Algozzine, B. (2011a). Leadership in education and the "vision" thing. *Multicultural Learning and Teaching, 6*(1), 1–4.

Obiakor, F. E., & Algozzine, B. (2011b). Beware of false prophets of multicultural education. *Multicultural Learning and Teaching, 6*(2), 1–6.

106 *Valuing Other Voices*

Obiakor, F. E., Banks, T., Rotatori, A. F., & Utley, C. (2017). *Leadership matters in the education of students with special needs in the 21st century*. Charlotte, NC: Information Age.

Obiakor, F. E., & Beachum, F. D. (2005). *Urban education for the 21st century: Research, issues, and perspectives*. Springfield, IL: Charles C. Thomas.

Obiakor, F. E., Enwefa, S., Utley, C., Obi, S. O., Gwalla-Ogisi, N., & Enwefa, R. (2004). *Serving culturally and linguistically diverse students with emotional and behavioral disorders*. Arlington, VA: Council for Children with Behavioral Disorders, the Council for Exceptional Children.

Obiakor F. E., & Ford, B. A. (2002). *Creating successful learning environments for African American learners with exceptionalities*. Thousand Oaks, CA: Corwin Press.

Obiakor, F. E., & Gordon, J. U. (2003). *African perspectives in American higher education: Invisible voices*. Hauppauge, NY: Nova Science.

Obiakor, F. E., & Grant, P. (2005). *Foreign-born African Americans: Silenced voices in the discourse on race*. Hauppauge, NY: Nova Science.

Obiakor, F. E., Grant, P. A., & Dooley, E. A. (2002). *Educating all learners: Refocusing the comprehensive support model*. Springfield, IL: Charles C. Thomas.

Obiakor, F. E., Grant, P., & Obi, S. O. (2010). *Voices of foreign-born African American teacher educators in the United States*. New York, NY: Nova Science.

Obiakor, F. E., Harris, M. K., & Beachum, F. D. (2009). The state of special education for African American learners in Milwaukee. In G. Williams & F. E. Obiakor (Eds.), *The state of education of urban learners and possible solutions: The Milwaukee experience* (pp. 31–48). Dubuque, IA: Kendall/Hunt.

Obiakor, F. E., & Martinez, J. (2018). *Latin@ voices in multicultural education: From invisibility to visibility in higher education*. New York, NY: Nova Science.

Obiakor, F. E., Mehring, T. A., & Schwenn, J. O. (1997). *Disruption, disaster, and death: Helping students deal with crises*. Reston, VA: The Council for Exceptional Children.

Obiakor, F. E., Schwenn, J. O., & Rotatori, A. F. (1999). *Advances in special education: Multicultural education for learners with exceptionalities* (Vol. 12). Stanford, CT: JAI Press.

Obiakor, F. E., & Stile, S. W. (1990). Enhancing self-concept in students of visually impaired and normally sighted middle school children. *Journal of Psychology, 12,* 199–206.

Obiakor, F. E., & Utley, C. A. (1997). Rethinking preservice preparation for teachers in the learning disabilities field: Workable multicultural strategies. *Learning Disabilities Research & Practice, 12,* 100–106.

Obiakor, F. E., Utley, C. A., & Rotatori, A. F. (2003). *Advances in special education: Effective education for learners with exceptionalities* (Vol. 15). Oxford, England: Elsevier Science/JAI Press.

Obiakor, F. E., & Wilder, L. K. (2003, October). Disproportionate representation in special education: What principals can do. *Principal Leadership, 4,* 17–21.

O'Brien, R. (2017). *Women presidents and prime Ministers: 2018 edition*. Washington, DC: Double Bridge.

Ogbu, J. U. (1978). *Minority education and caste*. San Francisco, CA: Academic Press.

References 107

Orfield, G., Ee, J., Frankenberg, E., & Siegel-Hawley, G. (2016). *Brown* at 62: School segregation by race, poverty and state, Civil Rights Project. Retrieved from https://escholarship.org/uc/item/5ds6k0rd

Paramount Pictures. (1988). *Coming to America*. Los Angeles, CA: Author.

Pennsylvania Association for Retarded Children v. Commonwealth of Pennsylvania, 343 F. Supp. 279 (D. C. Pa 1971).

Pew Research Center (2008). *U.S. Population Projections: 2005–2050*. Washington, DC: Author.

Prater, L. P. (2006, October). *Institutionalized terror: A social system's analysis of police brutality*. Paper presented at the annual professional development conference of the National Social Science Association, San Francisco, CA.

Price, H. B. (1991, Fall). Multicultural education: The debate. *Humanities in the South*, pp. 1–8.

Purkey, W. (1970). *Self-concept and school achievement*. Englewood Cliffs, NJ: Prentice Hall.

Rueda, R. (2007). Multicultural special education: Future perspectives. In F. E. Obiakor (Ed.), *Multicultural special education: Culturally responsive teac*hing (pp. 290–297). Upper Saddle River, NJ: Pearson/Merrill Prentice Hall.

Santrock, J. W., & Yussen, S R. (1989). *Child development: An introduction* (4th ed.). Dubuque, IA: Kendall Hunt.

Sasso, G. M. (2003, May). An examined life: A response to James Kauffman's reflections on the field. *Behavioral Disorders, 28*, 209–211.

Schrag, J. A. (1993). Restructuring schools for better alignment of general and special education. In J. I. Goolad & T. C. Lovitt (Eds.), *Integrating general and special education* (pp. 203–227). New York, NY: Merrill.

Shavelson, R., Bolus, R., & Keasling, J. (1980). Self-concept: Recent developments in theory and methods. In *New directions for testing and measurement* (pp. 23–43). New York, NY: Harper & Row.

Shoaf, N. L. (1990, October). Today's family: Is stress killing your kids? *The Plain Truth, 55*(9), 12–13.

Siconne, F., & Canfield, J. (19993). *101 ways to develop student self-esteem and responsibility* (vol. 2). Boston, MA: Allyn & Bacon.

Sin, R. H. (2017). *A beautiful composition of broken*. Kansas City, MO: Andrews McMeel.

Smith, D. D., & Tyler, N. C. (2010). *Introduction to special education: Making a difference* (7th ed.). Upper Saddle River, NJ: Merrill.

Smith, T. B., Richards, P. S., MacGranley, H., & Obiakor, F. E. (2004). Practicing multiculturalism: An introduction. In T. B. Smith (Ed.), *Practicing multiculturalism: Affirming diversity in counseling and psychology* (pp. 3–16). Boston: Allyn & Bacon.

Smith, T. E. (2005). IDEA 2004: Another round in the reauthorization process. *Remedial and Special Education, 26*(6), 314–323.

Snygg, F., & Combs, A. (1949). *Individual behavior*. New York, NY: Harper & Row.

Soyinka, W. (1994). *The man died: The prison notes of Wole Soyinka*. London, England: Random House.

Stein, G. (1937). *Everybody's autobiography*. Cambridge, MA: Exact Change.

108 *Valuing Other Voices*

Sue, D. W., & Sue, D. (2008). *Counseling the culturally diverse: Theory and practice* (5th ed.). Hoboken, NJ: John Wiley & Sons.

Summers, S. B. (2004, December). *Self-concept of academic ability among ninth grade students attending a private college preparatory high school.* Unpublished PhD dissertation, Urban Education Exceptional Education, University of Wisconsin-Milwaukee, Milwaukee, WI.

Tucker, A. (1984). *Chairing the academic department: Leadership among peers* (2nd ed.). New York, NY: American Council on Education.

Utley, C. A., & Obiakor, F. E. (2001). *Special education, multicultural education,* and school reform: Components of quality education for learners with mild *disabilities.* Springfield, IL: Charles C. Thomas.

Vocational Rehabilitation Act (1973), Pub. L. No. 93-112.

Wald, J. L. (1996). Diversity in the special education training force. *NCPSE News, 1*, 1, 6.

Walter J. Black. (1944). *The works of William Shakespeare.* Roslyn, NY: Black's Readers Service.

Weikart, D. P. (1977). Preschool intervention for the disadvantaged child: A challenge for special education. In H. H. Spicker, K. J. Anastasiow, & W. L. Hodges (Eds.), *Children with special needs: Early development and education* (pp. 73–89). Minneapolis, MN: Leadership Training Institute/Special Education, University of Minnesota.

Wilder, L. K., Obiakor, F. E., & Algozzine, B. (2003, Summer). Homeless students in special education: Beyond the myth of socioeconomic dissonance. *The Journal of At-Risk Issues, 9*, 9–16.

Winzer, M. A., & Mazurek, K. (1998). *Special education in multicultural contexts.* Upper Saddle River, NJ: Merrill/Prentice Hall.

Yell, M. L. (2004). *The law and special education* (2nd ed.). Upper Saddle River, NJ: Prentice Hall.

ABOUT THE AUTHOR

Festus E. Obiakor, PhD, is the chief executive manager, Sunny Educational Consulting, Shorewood, Wisconsin. His graduate degrees are from Texas Christian University, Fort Worth, Texas, and New Mexico State University, Las Cruces, New Mexico. He has served as a department head and professor, Valdosta State University, Valdosta, Georgia, and The City College of New York, New York. A teacher, scholar, leader, and consultant, he has served as distinguished visiting professor at a variety of universities. He is the author of more than 150 publications, including books, articles, and commentaries; and he has presented papers at many national and international conferences. He serves on the editorial boards of reputable nationally and internationally refereed journals, including *Multicultural Learning and Teaching* in which he serves as executive editor. Dr. Obiakor is a leader who has been involved in many landmark scholarly works in the fields of general and special education, with particular focus on African American and other culturally and linguistically diverse learners and he continues to prescribe multidimensional methods of assessment, teaching, and intervention for these individuals. Based on this premise, Dr. Obiakor created the comprehensive support model, an intervention model that values the collaborative, consultative, and cooperative energies of students, families, teachers/service providers, communities, and government agencies.

Printed in the United States
By Bookmasters